Politik und Wirtschaft – bilingual

herausgegeben von Amy Benzmann

Economic Globalisation

Amy Benzmann
Inka Hemmerich

C.C. Buchner Verlag · Bamberg

Politik und Wirtschaft– bilingual
herausgegeben von Amy Benzmann

Economic Globalisation

bearbeitet von:
Amy Benzmann und Inka Hemmerich

Zu diesem Lehrwerk sind erhältlich:
- Erwartungshorizonte zu den Aufgaben zum Download auf www.ccbuchner.de (BN 710532)

1. Auflage, 1. Druck 2017
Alle Drucke dieser Auflage sind, weil untereinander unverändert, nebeneinander benutzbar.

Dieses Werk folgt der reformierten Rechtschreibung und Zeichensetzung. Ausnahmen bilden Texte, bei denen künstlerische, philologische oder lizenzrechtliche Gründe einer Änderung entgegenstehen.

Die Eigentexte in diesem Werk folgen der britischen Schreibung.

Redaktion: Andreas Gerster
Grafische Gestaltung: HOCHVIER GmbH & Co. KG, Bamberg
Druck und Bindung: creo Druck- und Medienservice GmbH, Bamberg

www.ccbuchner.de

ISBN 978-3-661-71053-2

Vorwort

In der Schule hat **der bilinguale Unterricht** in den letzten Jahren stark an Bedeutung gewonnen. Als Fachunterricht in der Fremdsprache befähigt diese Unterrichtsform Schülerinnen und Schüler dazu, spezifische Sachverhalte in einer anderen Sprache zu erschließen, darzustellen und über Problemstellungen zu diskutieren. Neben der Sprachkompetenz wird auch die interkulturelle Kompetenz gefördert – eine wichtige Voraussetzung für das Bestehen in einem sprachlich und kulturell vielfältigen Europa und in einer global vernetzen Welt. Bilinguales Lernen vermittelt wichtige Kompetenzen und Fertigkeiten, die die Schülerinnen und Schüler auf ihr Studium und die zunehmend international ausgerichtete Berufswelt vorbereiten.

Unsere **neue Reihe „Politik und Wirtschaft – bilingual"** bietet thematisch abgeschlossene Module in englischer Sprache, die Sie flexibel im Unterricht einsetzen können. Die aktuellen und multiperspektivisch gestalteten Materialien in der Zielsprache unterstützen die Schülerinnen und Schüler dabei, ihre fachlichen, kommunikativen und methodischen Kompetenzen weiterzuentwickeln und regen zum Perspektivwechsel und zur kritischen Auseinandersetzung mit aktuellen internationalen Entwicklungen und Fragestellungen an.

Das vorliegende Arbeitsheft **„Economic Globalisation"** eignet sich für den Einsatz in den höheren Jahrgangsstufen der Sekundarstufen I und in der Sekundarstufe II. Vor allem Fragen der Gerechtigkeit und des Wohlstandes der Menschen werden heute mit den Auswirkungen der ökonomischen Globalisierung in Verbindung gebracht. In der politischen Debatte ist dabei aber häufig eine erschreckende Unkenntnis über die Hintergründe und Gestaltungsmöglichkeiten der ökonomischen Globalisierung festzustellen. Das Heft fordert dazu auf, sich ein eigenes Urteil zu bilden. Überwiegend an Fallbeispielen werden die komplexen Ursachen, Auswirkungen und Zusammenhänge der ökonomischen Globalisierung beleuchtet. Das Heft schließt mit einem Ausblick auf die Notwendigkeit, globale ökonomische Probleme mit Hilfe globaler Institutionen zu bearbeiten.

Das Konzept des Heftes

- Jedes Unterkapitel enthält eine Sammlung von anschaulichen Materialien und Texten, die mit Hilfe von Arbeitsaufträgen („Exercises") erschlossen werden können.

- In der Randspalte befinden sich Begriffserläuterungen, Vokabelerklärungen und weiterführende Hinweise zu den Themen.

- Der Serviceteil enthält eine Sammlung nützlicher Redemittel für die Diskussion in der Klasse.

Das Autorenteam wünscht Ihnen neue Einsichten und fruchtbare Diskussionen bei der Auseinandersetzung mit diesem spannenden Thema!

Table of Contents

1. The World as a Global Village?

1.1 What is Globalisation?

M 1 We Got these Cool Hats in Niketown in Paris ...

Cartoon: Matt Wuerker

M 2 What is Globalisation?

Globalisation is the process of interaction and integration among people, companies, and governments of different nations, a process driven by international trade, investment and aided by technology. This process effects the environment, culture, political systems, economic development and prosperity. In general, globalisation can be seen as the widening, intensifying, speeding up, and growing impact of world-wide interconnectedness.

Globalisation itself is not a new development. Trade between countries has taken place for thousands of years, from the Silk Road connecting China and Europe during the Middle Ages to companies and countries investing abroad. What is new however, is the dramatic increase in speed and volume of international trade in the last 200 years, especially in the second half of the 20th century.

Technological inventions in the transportation as well as in the information and communication sector is one reason for globalisation. Another cause is the adoption of free-market economic systems by a growing number of countries. Furthermore, there was a decrease in international regulations and tariffs between 1950–2000. By opening their economies new opportunities for international trade have been created.

Globalisation today affects all areas of life,

from buying imported products to chatting with friends abroad online. The average global citizen watches American movies, eats Japanese Sushi, wears clothes sewn in Vietnam and uses a mobile produced in China. Even though many people feel more connected by globalisation, it is also controversial. For example, European trade policies affect African states, new germs and viruses are able to spread faster than ever before and "mcdonaldisation" is changing local cultures. While supporters of globalisation claim that free trade leads to economic development and higher living standards all over the world, opponents of globalisation argue that mainly rich countries, and especially international corporations, benefit from the free market at the expense of poor countries and common people.

M 3 Opinions About Globalisation

[Globalisation] has enriched the world scientifically and culturally and benefited many people economically as well. *Amartya Sen*

If globalisation is to succeed, it must succeed for poor and rich alike. It must deliver rights no less than riches. It must provide social justice and equity no less than economic prosperity and enhanced communication. *Kofi Annan*

We, the people of the Earth, are one large family. The new epoch offers new challenges and new global problems, such as environmental catastrophes, exhaustion of resources, bloody conflicts and poverty. *Eduard Shevardnadze*

Amartya Kumar Sen
born 3rd November 1933, is an Indian economist and philosopher, who was awarded the Nobel Memorial Prize in Economic Sciences in 1998. His main topics are welfare economics, social choice theory and economic and social justice as well as economic theory of famines and indexes of the measure of well-being of citizens of developing countries.

Kofi Atta Annan
born 8th April 1938, is a Ghanaian diplomat. He was the seventh Secretary-General of the United Nations from 1997 to 2006 and in process, along with the UN, was awarded the Nobel Peace Prize in 2001.

Eduard Amvrosiyevich Shevardnadze
(25th January 1928 – 7th July 2014) was a Georgian politician and diplomat. In his role as First Secretary of the Georgian Communist Party (GPC) he was de facto the leader of Soviet Georgia from 1972 to 1985 and President of Georgia from 1992 to 2003.

Exercises

1. Explain what the cartoon has to do with globalisation (M 1).
2. Create an "ABC" about how you and your family are affected by globalisation in everyday life. Use as many letters of the alphabet as possible. For example: A – American products, I – international travel, M – McDonald's ... Compare your results with a partner.
3. Create a poster explaining globalisation to other students. Use the information given in this section as well as pictures from magazines, newspapers etc. (M 2).
4. Discuss the quotes above. Which one do you (dis)agree with most? Give reason (M 3).

1.2 Dimensions and Indicators of Globalisation

M 4 ● Snap-shots of Globalisation

VW-cars ready for shipping overseas

McDonald's restaurant in China

Young protester against WTO

Flood in Venice – an effect of global climate change?

M 5 ● Dimensions of Globalisation

Globalisation has several dimensions: an economic one, a political one, an ecological as well as a socio-cultural one (the last one is sometimes even seen as two different dimensions). They are deeply connected, with varying intersections, and cannot be viewed separatly. However, defining the dimensions helps to grasp the concept of globalisation more easily.

- The economic dimension refers to (the increase of) international trade as well as international capital investments. Production is often transnationally integrated, mostly run by multinational companies that in some cases generate higher revenues than small states. On the other hand, many countries unite in economic associations or unions like the ASEAN or the European Union.
- The ecological dimension: Often locally induced ecological problems have global effects such as global warming or the clearing of rainforests. For example, smaller island states are under high threat by rising sea levels as a result of global warming. These states depend on the international community acting together. Therefore, in order to address issues like these, states are looking more and more for trans- or international solutions through forums like the Paris United Nations Climate Conference in 2015.

ASEAN = Association of East Asian Nations

international = between or among nations; involving two or more nations

transnational = going beyond national boundaries or interests

- The political dimension: Similarly, many political problems can only be successfully addressed internationally or globally. For example, militant conflicts such as the one in Syria, often spread to other countries and affect the rest of the world in multiple ways. Terrorists often hunker down in weakened or failed states and waves of refugees can destabilise neighbouring areas or regions. Transnational organisations like the European Union or the United Nations try to find global solutions to issues such as these.
- The socio-cultural dimension: Modern information and communication technologies enable people all over the world to talk to each other and connect at unmatched low prices. Furthermore, consumer products that are available globally do affect local cultures. For example, the show "Who wants to be a Millionaire" can be seen in over 100 states all over the world.

M 6 How to Measure Globalisation

Economic globalisation indicators provide an overview of the main trends in globalisation. They are based on data already available in the Eurostat database and have been constructed so that they can be meaningfully compared across countries. There are five groups in which a total of twelve indicators were presented in June 2014:

- International trade: Share of imports of goods and services in % of GDP, share of exports of goods and services in % of GDP, export to import ratio.
- Foreign direct investment (FDI): share of inward FDI stocks in % of GDP, share of outward FDI stocks in % of GDP, FDI flows intensity – market integration.
- Employment: Employment in foreign controlled enterprises as a share of total domestic employment, employment development in foreign controlled enterprises, employment development in foreign affiliates of domestic enterprises.
- Research and development (R&D): R&D expenditure in foreign controlled enterprises as a share of total R&D expenditure.
- Value added: Value added in foreign controlled enterprises as a share of total value added, value added development in foreign controlled enterprises.

© European Union 2017, http://ec.europa.eu/eurostat/web/economic-globalisation-indicators/indicators (29.3.2017)

constructing data = gathering data systematically

affiliates = foreign subsidiary company

value added = value that is created by the company for example by producing or assembling specific parts or goods (Wertschöpfung)

M 7 Global Internet Users

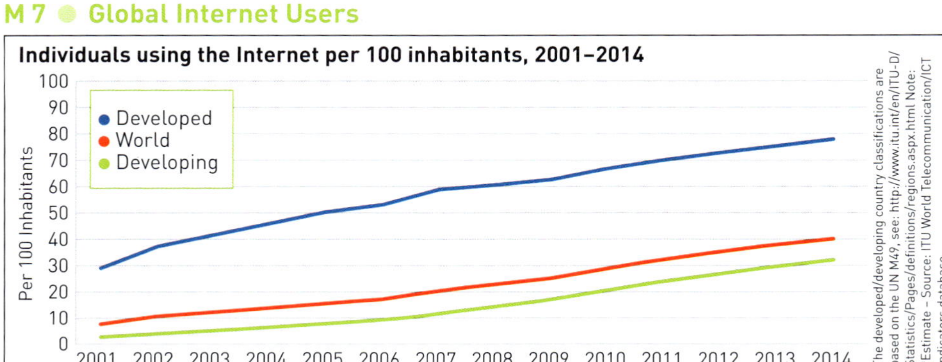

M 8 Development of International Trade

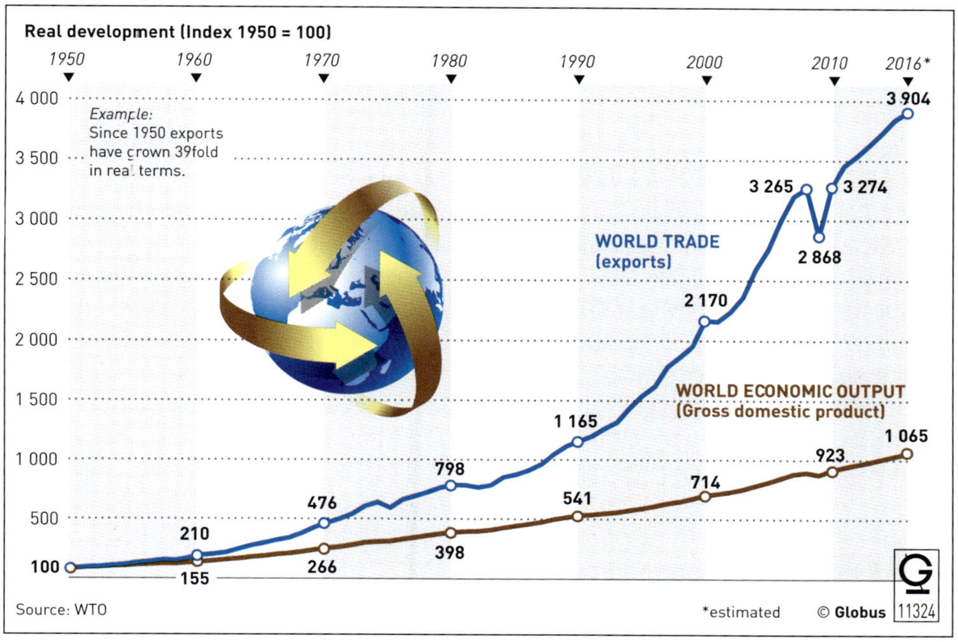

Gross domestic product (GDP) =
measures all final goods and services produced in a specific country or region in a specific period of time (quarterly or yearly) in order to determine the economic performance and standard of living as well as make international comparisons.

M 9 Globalisation Backlash 2.0

The first great era of globalisation in the 19th century saw the share of trade in global GDP rise eightfold between 1820 and 1913. The emergence of the railway and steamship allowed bulky products to be sent speedily across borders. British freight rates fell by 70% between 1840 and 1890. No longer did international trade have to focus on high value goods like silks and spices. Capital also flowed across borders with British savers helping to finance railway construction in Latin America and elsewhere. Mass migration was another phenomenon of the late 19th and early 20th centuries; Europeans emigrated at a rate of 300,000 a year in the first three decades after 1846, and over 1m a year between 1900 and 1914. On the eve of the First World War, foreign born people comprised 15% of the populations of America and Canada; by 1965, just 6%.

The war brought an abrupt end to the trend. But there were signs of a backlash even before the guns started firing in August 1914. Britain was wracked with a period of civil and industrial strife dubbed "the strange death of Liberal England"; strikes on the railways and in the mines; and an effective mutiny in northern Ireland. Both Germany and Russia saw the war as a way of enhancing patriotism and countering the rising power of socialism. [...]

Were the events linked? Globalisation means that prices for commodities tend to be driven by international, rather than local, forces. [...] In short, globalisation can mean rapid change in industries and across economies; change that many people find it difficult to adjust to. While economists talk of retraining and mobility, many people would rather stick to what they know and where they live. So they resist that change or look for someone (foreigners, minorities) to blame (Karl Lueger, an anti-semite, was elected mayor of Vienna three times before the First World War). [...] In his book "The Globalisation Paradox", Dani Rodrik suggested that "we cannot simulta-

wrack =
plague, torture

bulky =
voluminous, big

mutiny =
uproar, riot

commodities =
goods

neously pursue democracy, national determination and economic globalisation. If we want to push globalisation further, we have to give up either the nation state or democratic politics."

In theory, we could combine globalisation with international democracy (giving up the nation state) but as your blogger has pointed out before, politicians are stuck between voter demands for local control and the international forces that shape economies. When they try to cooperate–on trade deals, for example–they are accused of selling out to corporate interests or other states. The Brexit vote in the UK was a rebellion against international co-operation, with the loss of local sovereignty that implies.

Luckily, the reaction against globalisation needn't lead to world war this time (although political violence seems to be increasing). Still, the prospects are worrying. That is because a feedback process can set in; terrorism can lead to repression, which inspires more recruits to terrorism [...]. And it is also because economic nationalism leads to the kind of "eye for an eye" process that makes everyone worse off. Already world trade growth is in the doldrums; [...] Things may get worse. [...]

So the feedback is that angry voters back nationalist politicians, whose policies further impoverish those voters, who become even angrier and so on. Now of course one can retort that pro-globalisation politicians have failed to ensure that workers have enjoyed the fruits of trade growth. But they will enjoy a trade slump even less.

Philipp Coggan (Buttonwood), http://www.economist.com/blogs/buttonwood/2016/07/economics-and-politics-0 (29.3.2017)

doldrums = downfall, regression

retort = reply, counter

slump = fall, drop

Exercises

1. Create a mind map about globalisation using the four dimensions as single branches (M 4, M 5).
2. Discuss in groups how the indicators named in M 6 can contribute to measuring globalisation.
3. Analyse the infographics in M 7/M 8. What information do they show?
4. Compare and contrast the reasons that led to an economic backlash at the beginning of the 20th century and today (M 9). Create a Venn-Diagram, writing similarities in the overlapping part of the circles and differences in the other parts.
5. Project: For a week, collect everything you can find about globalisation, e.g. pictures, headlines ..., and assign it to one of the four dimensions.

Venn-Diagramm

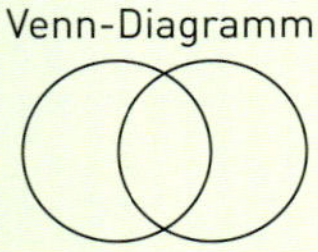

2. The Economic Dimension of Globalisation

2.1 Does Free Trade Benefit All?

M 1 ● Free Trade at Last ...

Cartoon: Khalid Bendib

M 2 ● Free Trade Agreements Around the World

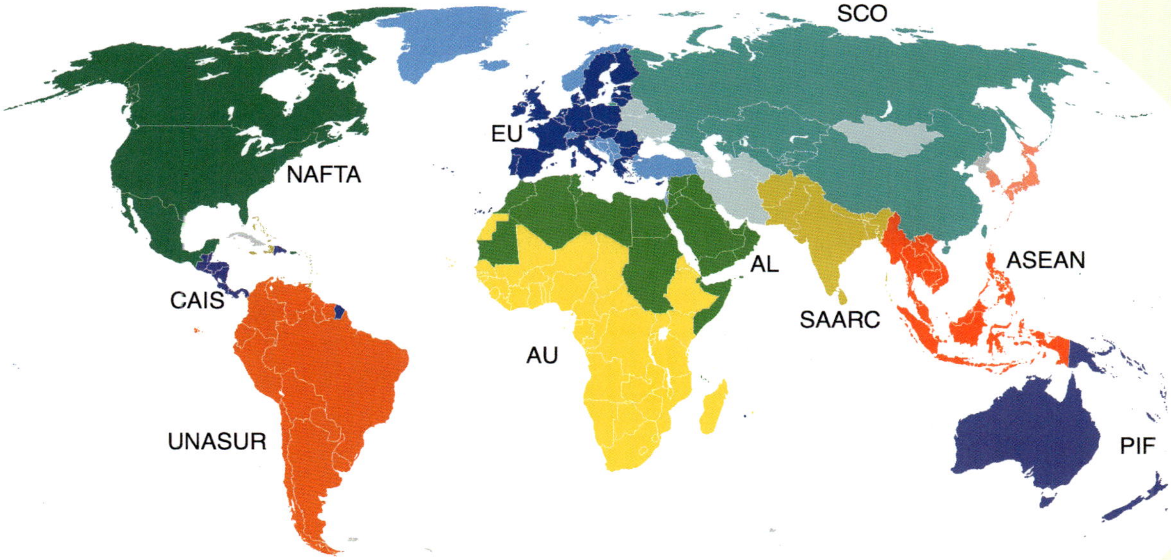

FTAA =
Free Trade Area of the Americas; proposed agreement to eliminate or reduce the trade barriers among all countries in the Americas, negotiations were unsuccessful

WTO =
World Trade Organisation, see M 4

M 3 Free Trade vs. Protectionism

a) The advantages of free trade

Free trade is an economic theory that describes the import and export relations of multiple countries. Countries engage in free trade relations when companies and individuals can import and export goods free from government intervention. Government intervention can include tariffs, import limits and/or bans on specific goods. Free trade offers several advantages to countries. [...]

Lower costs

Free trade allows companies to lower their business costs by using the cheapest economic resources available. Traditionally, free trade allows companies to import raw materials for producing business goods domestically. Companies can also make direct investments into foreign economies to produce goods at a lower cost in these environments. Goods manufactured in foreign countries can then be exported to domestic economies with little to no government intervention. Business technology also allows companies to outsource service departments, such as technical support or customer service, to foreign countries. [...]

Increase in Purchasing Power

Nations engaging in free trade can also increase the purchasing power of businesses and individuals. Businesses may choose to purchase goods from a foreign country if significant advantages exist from foreign currency exchange rates. Fluctuating currency rates offer businesses a way to consistently offer low price goods to consumers. Even though companies can produce certain goods domestically, favorable currency exchange rates can provide companies with better purchase opportunities. Foreign goods may also allow companies to increase their profits by taking advantage of currency exchange rates.

Comparative Advantage

Comparative advantage is the economic theory that countries can produce a certain type of good better than other countries. This theory often lies in the fact that nations can have more natural resources than another country. Countries can also have a large labor pool or other technical abilities for producing consumer goods. A comparative advantage usually allows countries to maximize the production efficiency of their labor force. Creating highly desirable goods allows nations to generate high profits from exporting these items through the use of free trade agreements with other countries.

Improves Economic Growth

Free trade usually allows nations to improve their economic growth opportunities. Rather than relying on the fixed number of individuals in their domestic economy, countries can engage in free trade to improve business opportunities. Smaller countries may need to engage in free trade to acquire economic resources for producing consumer goods or services. Emerging economic environments also present high profit potential for companies exporting goods through free trade. Emerging economies often have consumers or businesses looking to purchase copious amounts of resources for production or consumption purposes.

Osmond Vitez, Leaf Group, Ltd. USA, http://smallbusiness.chron.com/pros-trade-3827.html (29.3.2017)

b) Reasons for protective behavior

Trade protection is the deliberate attempt to limit imports or promote exports by putting up barriers to trade. Despite the arguments in favor of free trade and increasing trade openness, protectionism is still widely practised. The main arguments for protection are:

Protect sunrise industries

Barriers to trade can be used to protect sunrise industries, also known as infant industries, such as those involving new technologies. This gives new firms the chance to develop, grow, and become globally competitive. [...]

Protect sunset industries

At the other end of scale are sunset industries, also known as declining industries, which might need some support to enable them to decline slowly, and avoid some of the negative effects of such decline. [...]

Protect strategic industries

Barriers may also be erected to protect strategic industries, such as energy, water, steel, armaments, and food. The implicit aim of the EUs Common Agricultural Policy is to create food security for Europe by protecting its agricultural sector.

Protect non-renewable resources

Non-renewable resources, including oil, are regarded as a special case where the normal rules of free trade are often abandoned. For countries aiming to rely on oil exports lasting into the long term, such as the oil-rich Middle Eastern economies, limiting output in the short term through production quotas is one method employed to conserve resources.

Deter unfair competition

Barriers may be erected to deter unfair competition, such as dumping by foreign firms at prices below cost.

Save jobs

Protecting an industry may, in the short run, protect jobs, though in the long run it is unlikely that jobs can be protected indefinitely.

Help the environment

Some countries may protect themselves from trade to help limit damage to their environment, such as that arising from CO_2 emissions caused by increased production and transportation.

Limit over-specialisation

Many economists point to the dangers of over-specialisation [...]. Retaining some self-sufficiency is seen as a sensible economic strategy given the risks of global downturns, and an over-reliance on international trade.
In addition to the economic arguments for protection, some protection may be for political reasons.

Richard Howarth, http://www.economicsonline.co.uk/Global_economics/Trade_protectionism.html (23.3.2017)

Non-Tariff Barriers to Trade

- Import bans
- General or product-specific quotas
- Quality conditions imposed by the importing country on the exporting countries
- Unreasonable/unjustified packaging, labelling, product standards
- Additional trade documents like Certificate of Origin, Certificate of Authenticity etc
- Export subsidies
- Fixation of a minimum import price
- "Buy national" policy
- Over-valued currency
- Corrupt and/or lengthy customs procedures

http://www.tradebarriers.org/ntb/non_tariff_barriers (3.2.2017)

The Principles of the WTO

The trading system should be ...

- without discrimination — a country should not discriminate between its trading partners (giving them equally "most-favoured-nation" or MFN status); and it should not discriminate between its own and foreign products, services or nationals (giving them "national treatment");
- freer — barriers coming down through negotiation;
- predictable — foreign companies, investors and governments should be confident that trade barriers (including tariffs and non-tariff barriers) should not be raised arbitrarily; tariff rates and market-opening commitments are "bound" in the WTO;
- more competitive — discouraging "unfair" practices such as export subsidies and dumping products at below cost to gain market share;
- more beneficial for less developed countries — giving them more time to adjust, greater flexibility, and special privileges.

© World Trade Organisation (WTO) 2017 / https://www.wto.org/english/thewto_e/whatis_e/tif_e/fact2_e.htm (20.2.2017)

M 4 ● The WTO

The World Trade Organization (WTO) is the international organization that oversees trade among member nations and acts as a forum for governments to negotiate trade agreements and settle trade disputes under a system of rules and procedures. Its aim is to increase world trade by lowering barriers to the international sale of goods and services, including intellectual property. The WTO was formed on January 1, 1995, replacing the postwar multilateral trading order under the General Agreement on Tariffs and Trade (GATT) with a more formal institutional arrangement. Headquartered in Geneva, Switzerland, the WTO as March 2017 had 164 members, the latest addition being Vietnam. The governing principles of the WTO's global trading system were described by Director General Pascal Lamy in 2006: "Built up stone by stone over the past 50 years, this system is founded on the idea that prosperity depends on efficiency, stability, predictability, and equity in international trade".

© International Encyclopedia of the Social Siences 2008, Thomson Gale / http://www.encyclopedia.com/social-sciences-and-law/political-science-and-government/international-organizations/world-trade (31.3.2017)

M 5 ● TTIP – and the Hassle that Came with it ...

London's Conway Hall was the venue for a Guardian Membership event held to debate the pros and cons of TTIP. The discussion was chaired by Guardian economics editor Larry Elliott and the panel comprised Claude Moraes, Labour MEP; Owen Tudor, head of European Union and International Relations, TUC; John Hilary, executive director of charity War on Want; and Vicky Pryce, chief economic adviser at the Centre for Economics and Business Research.

TTIP is a rather benign-sounding acronym, standing for the Transatlantic Trade and Investment Partnership. Still in the offing, TTIP is a deal between the EU and the US aimed at making it easier for the world's two biggest economies to trade. With 820m consumers and 60 % of global GDP between them, American and European economies could both increase by 0.5 percentage points from TTIP.

However, TTIP will not just make trade easier with tariff reduction; it is also set to remove a number of regulations that divide the US and the EU so the standards are harmonised between the two markets. [...]

As Vicky Pryce put it, "There is nothing wrong with increasing trade but it's how you go about it that is important."

TTIP will most likely benefit many industries in the EU and US – including pharmaceutical, energy, clothing and textiles, and food and drink. There will be a number of goods and services that the UK will be able to export for the first time – for example, British venison and lamb, which is banned in the US – and it will remove tariffs on exports, such as clothing produced in the EU.

"If we can build cars for the European market that don't need to be modified in Europe, which can also be sold in the US, well, that is going to benefit us hugely," Pryce said.

venue = meeting place

benign = kind, friendly

venison = collective name for deer, wild pig ...

So... what's the problem? First off, standards between the US and EU need to be harmonised, which will involve some rather picky changes – one example Larry Elliott gave was deciding where fire extinguishers will be placed on newly manufactured speedboats – and some big ones, such as redefining labour standards, environmental protections and standards of goods and services in the EU and across the Atlantic.

"Establishing standards for things like labour and safety, [TTIP] could also give us the ability to push and increase standards around the world," Pryce said. "If you think US standards are low, you should see some other places around the world."

John Hilary doesn't agree. "TTIP is about reaching behind the barriers and removing the standards and rules big business don't like dealing with, like labour standards, environmental standards, food safety standards," he said. "The EU is pushing to an end to port inspections of imports and exports, for example, which could lead to food safety problems."

In the UK, there are worries about the potential privatisation of treasured public services – education, transport, water, the NHS – and that this could lead to US companies running British institutions. [...]

There are environmental issues too: an estimated 11m extra tonnes of carbon dioxide will be produced if TTIP happens, and our reliance on fossil fuels will increase if it becomes easier for the US to export shale gas. According to John Hilary, this will all lead to "sub-saharan Africa getting it in the teeth". And your Parma ham and Champagne might be about to get a bit worse. What? Say it isn't so!

Cornish pasties from Colorado? I know. I've seen what Americans call cheese; it simply won't do. One contentious part of TTIP is that Europe wants its geographically-specific food stuffs, such as Champagne and Parma ham, to retain their protected status, which America apparently finds "a little bit surprising". There is room for amendments to TTIP: Brussels has asked retain the above protections and the French government asked to keep audio-visual services exempt, so the French film industry can be preserved in the face of the behemoth Hollywood machine.

So will TTIP ever become a reality? Because all 28 members of the EU will have to agree to TTIP and a number of countries have voiced concerns – mainly Germany, Austria, France and the UK – all of the members of the panel doubted to various degrees whether the treaty would become a reality [...].

Sian Caine, 18 Feb 2015, https://www.theguardian.com/membership/2015/feb/18/guardian-live-what-is-ttip-and-how-does-it-affect-us, (20.3.2017)

Current Status of TTIP
Since the 2016 US presidential election and the last round of talks between the EU and US, TTIP's fate is uncertain. Shortly after taking office in January 2017, President Trump signed an executive order ending the TPP (Transatlantic Pacific Partnership) free trade agreement between the US and Asia. Since President Trump's actions no large events have taken place to continue talks on TTIP. On the other hand no official action has been taken to actively end the negotiations between the US and the EU. (1.4.2017)

NHS =
National Health Service

getting it in the teeth =
a slap in the face

behemoth =
gigantic

Exercises

1. Analyse the cartoon in M 1.
2. Additional Research: Choose one of the trade agreements shown in M 2 and find more information about it (members, years of establishment, main conflicts, goal(s), etc.).
3. Compare and contrast the economic advantages of free trade and protectionism in the form of a table (M 3).
4. Explain how the WTO tries to increase world trade (M 4).
5. In class have a pro-con debate about TTIP. In preparation use M 3 and M 5.

2.2 Do Global Players Dominate the World Economy?

M 6 The Biggest Corporations of the World

Rank	Name	Industry	Revenue (USD million 2016)	Employees	Country
1	Walmart	Retail	$485,870	2,300,000	USA
2	State Grid	Electric utility	$329,601	927,839	CHN
3	China National Petroleum	Oil and gas	$299,271	1,589,508	CHN
4	Sinopec Group	Oil and gas	$294,344	810,538	CHN
5	Royal Dutch Shell	Oil and gas	$272,156	90,000	NED/GB
6	Exxon Mobil	Oil and gas	$246,204	75,600	USA
7	Volkswagen	Automotive	$236,600	610,070	GER
8	Toyota	Automotive	$236,592	348,877	JAP
9	Apple	Consumer electronics	$233,715	110,000	USA
10	BP	Oil and gas	$225,982	79,800	GB
11	Berkshire Hathaway	Conglomerate	$210,821	331,000	USA
12	McKesson	Health care	$192,487	68,000	USA
13	Samsung Electronics	Conglomerate	$177,440	319,000	KOR
14	Glencore	Commodities	$170,497	102,388	SUI
15	Industrial & Commercial Bank of China	Financial services	$167,227	466,346	CHN

Wikipedia, 31.7.2017

M 7 What are TNCs?

The effects of globalisation have enabled corporations to organise their production, trade and investments within so-called global value chains (GVCs) where the different stages of the production process are located across different countries. Globalisation therefore motivates companies to restructure their operations internationally through outsourcing and offshoring of activities using comparative price advantages for their own benefit.
Especially big firms have the ability to optimise their production processes by locating the various stages across different sites. The past decades thus have witnessed a strong trend towards the international dispersion of value chain activities such as design, production, marketing, distribution, etc.
When a foreign company invests in a country, perhaps by building a factory or a shop, this is called inward investment. Companies that operate in several countries are called multinational corporations (MNCs) or transnational corporations (TNCs). The US fast-food chain McDonald's is a large MNC – it has nearly 30,000 restaurants in 119 countries.

Factors attracting TNCs to a country may include:
- cheap raw materials
- cheap labour supply
- good transport
- low taxes
- less environmental requirements
- access to markets where the goods are sold
- friendly government policies

M 8 Positive and Negative Impacts of MNCs

A key feature of the process of globalisation has been the increasing impact of MNCs as they expand their operations into more than one country. What is the overall balance of this impact?

The potential benefits of MNCs on host countries include:

- Provision of significant employment and training to the labour force in the host country
- Transfer of skills and expertise, helping to develop the quality of the host labour force
- MNCs add to the host country GDP through their spending, for example with local suppliers and through capital investment
- Competition from MNCs acts as an incentive to domestic firms in the host country to improve their competitiveness, perhaps by raising quality and/or efficiency
- MNCs extend consumer and business choice in the host country
- Profitable MNCs are a source of significant tax revenues for the host economy (for example on profits earned as well as payroll and sales-related taxes)

The potential drawbacks of MNCs on host countries include:

- Domestic businesses may not be able to compete with MNCs and some will fail
- MNCs may not feel that they need to meet the host country expectations for acting ethically and/or in a socially-responsible way
- MNCs may be accused of imposing their culture on the host country, perhaps at the expense of the richness of local culture. Might MNCs reduce cultural diversity around the world as they continue to expand, particularly into less developed or developing countries?
- Profits earned by MNCs may be remitted back to the MNC's base country rather than reinvested in the host economy.
- MNCs may make use of transfer pricing and other tax avoidance measures to significant reduce the profits on which they pay tax to the government in the host country.

Jim Riley, https://www.tutor2u.net/business/reference/impact-of-multinational-companies-mncs-on-their-host-countries (3.4.2017)

M 9 China's Investment in Africa

Helen Hai, vice-president of Chinese footwear manufacturer the Huajian Group, has a bold ambition. Within a decade, she wants Ethiopia to be a global hub for the shoe industry, supplying the African, European and American markets.

„We are not coming all the way here just to reduce our costs by 10 to 20 %," Hai says. „Our aim is in 10 years' time to have a new cluster of shoe making here. We want to build a whole supply chain ... I want everything to be produced here."

Huajian has a factory near Addis Ababa employing 600 people, which opened in January 2012, and has committed to jointly invest $2bn (£1.3bn) over the next decade to create a light manufacturing special economic zone in Ethiopia, creating employment for around 100,000 Ethiopians. The company, which employs 25,000 workers in China, expects to be able to provide around 30,000 jobs in Addis Ababa by 2022.

Huajian's partner in this project is the China-Africa Development Fund (CADFund), a private equity facility promoting Chinese investment in the continent. Born out of the

2006 Forum on China-Africa Co-operation, the fund was launched in June 2007 with $1bn provided by the China Development Bank. A further injection of $2bn was made early last year.

CADFund focuses on funding agriculture, infrastructure, natural resources and industrial park projects like that planned by Huajian, and has invested in a diverse range of ventures including a power plant in Ghana, a port in Nigeria, cotton farms in Malawi and a $100m car plant in South Africa.

Hai's vision is on its way to becoming a reality: a lease has been signed on 300 hectares (741 acres) of land in Lebu, on the outskirts of Addis Ababa, where Huajian plans to build a „shoe city", providing accommodation for up to 200,000 workers and factory space for other producers of footwear, handbags and accessories. The complex will offer help and advice to entrepreneurs setting up companies. „[It will be] a one-stop shop for manufacturers that are similar to us," Hai, who expects construction on the site to begin this year, says. „One thing in my strategy is very clear: that I don't want to compete with locals," Hai says. „I want to help them grow because when local producers grow, the whole market is growing. If it is just myself growing here in five years' time, I will leave."

One area where she feels the company could make a difference is in leather tanning. „The sheepskin and goatskin are good but local people don't know how to manage cowskin," Hai says. „I want to offer my skills to help the locals. I don't want to have my own tannery because I don't want to create problems. I want to be friendly."

This kind of warm and fuzzy talk from a Chinese company may surprise some analysts, academics and journalists who often characterise China's involvement in Africa as voracious neocolonial pillaging. Hai admits that her strategy is not necessarily pursued by every Chinese private enterprise operating in the continent.

Zemedeneh Negatu, managing partner at Ernst & Young Ethiopia, welcomes Huajian's

lease = rental agreement

voracious = greedy

pillage = raid, plunder

Ethiopian factory workers make shoes at the Chinese company Huajian's plant in Addis Ababa, Ethiopia.

plan to build a complete supply chain for the shoe industry and applauds its efforts to transfer skills. „That should be the goal. You create clusters around one or two major foreign or Ethiopian investors, throughout the country, based on competitive and comparative advantages," he says. „Huajian could be the anchor but all around are Ethiopian companies. It should be made clear to investors that they need to help build local capacity."

The company cites employee welfare as a priority. In China, Huajian has a modest outfit 40km (25 miles) south of the capital, Beijing, employing 1,700 workers and exporting more than $1m worth of shoes each month to the US and the UK. In Dongguan, in the southern province of Guangdong, the majority of the staff come from poor rural areas. The company provides accommodation, hot meals, clothing and laundry services, as well as free childcare. A similar package is offered to its Ethiopian workers who, in addition, earn 10 % above the average local wage.

The Huajian factory near Addis Ababa employs 130 Chinese workers, all in supervisory roles. The number of expatriates on the payroll has come down from 200 when production began in January 2012, and Huajian plans to reduce it further. „For me, localisation is so important. I don't see myself managing this factory in five to eight years' time. I see someone local standing here talking to you," Hai says.

The company has selected 130 university graduates from southern Ethiopia to spend a year in China at its training facility. About 270 more will be recruited later. „They are going to be the future managers," Hai says. „They are going to be a new force."

Elissa Jobson in Addis Ababa, The Guardian, 30 Apr 2013 (10.8.2017)

Exercises

1. Divide into 5 groups.
   a) Compare the revenue of the biggest corporations to the GDP of Germany, the US, Kenya and Vietnam (M 6).
   b) Summarise the main characteristics of a TNC (M 7).
   c) Additional Research: Choose one of the top 10 TNCs in the table (M 6). Your research should include: general information on the TNC, their sales volume, global value chains, revenue, number of employees and the number of foreign representations.
2. List the advantages and disadvantages of TNCs/MNCs in the form of a table (M 8). Add your own findings.
3. Outline the African perspective on China's investments in Africa (M 9).
4. A Chinese textile company wants to open a factory in Ethiopia. Consult the Ethiopian government on whether or not they should allow the textile company to build a factory (M 6 – M 9).

2.3 How can Germany Compete Globally?

Global Competitiveness Index 2015

1	Switzerland
2	Singapore
3	United States
4	Netherlands
5	Germany
6	Sweden
7	United Kingdom
8	Japan
9	Hongkong
10	Finnlands

diversified = here: having many different areas of research and forms of research

per capita = per head

SME = small and medium enterprises

leading lights = here: leading and innovative companies in their field

R&D = Research and Development

gross pay = money earned before taxes and other expenses

non-wage labour costs = employer costs for things like insurance contributions, additional days off, retirement, maternity leave, etc.

patent = an official government document which gives the inventor the right to sell, manufacture or use the invention for a certain number of years.

M 10 ● Competing for Business

Big corporations today can choose locations for their facilities globally, looking for the best access to customers, workers, transportation, etc. Nations compete for industries as they can bring technology, investment and jobs. In this competitive environment, countries try to attract firms with low interest rates for investment, good governance, guaranteed property rights and skilled and motivated workers.

For commercial success and competitive advantage the following location factors among others are important for corporations. However, the importance of the factors depends on the kind of industry:

- availability of raw materials and energy
- proximity to market
- infrastructural facilities
- supporting industries and services
- government policy, regulations and taxation
- availability of skilled manpower
- ecological and environmental factors
- climatic conditions

M 11 ● Industry's Competitiveness: How is Germany Doing?

Germany has managed to safeguard its strong industrial base, even in this globalisation age – with international locations competing with each other, and companies responding to unfavourable conditions by relocating first production and even business sites themselves. This is because of the multiple geographical advantages that make industrial production in Germany attractive from an international perspective. These advantages include a large domestic market at the heart of Europe and a mainly modern energy, transport and telecommunications infrastructure (...) a motivated and skilled workforce plus a diversified and productive research environment, a high number of businesses per capita and a varied structure in terms of size and sector, with an efficient industrial SME sector including leading lights in many niche areas ("hidden champions"); thus enabling the formation of networks and clusters, a very high percentage, by international standards, of R&D-intensive industries; traditionally, German industry excels in sophisticated technology, e.g. automotive and mechanical engineering, the chemical industry and electrical engineering, but it has also made significant gains in cutting-edge technologies and developed particular expertise in the area of medical devices and instrumentation, high productivity in the manufacturing sector (...). However, there is no hiding from the fact that Germany faces major challenges in a number of areas, particularly the following: compared internationally, German industry must tolerate high labour costs (gross pay and non-wage labour costs) and high electricity and energy costs, a skills shortage is becoming an increasingly urgent problem; (...) in contrast to other countries such as the US and China, the number of patent applications has been stagnating for years in Germany (...)

http://www.bmwi.de/English/Redaktion/Pdf/germany-industry-nation,property=pdf,bereich=bmwi,sprache=en,rwb=true.pdf, (15.5.2017)

M 12 Germany on the Global Competitiveness Index

Germany 5th / 138

Performance overview

	Rank/138	Score (1–7)
Global Competitiveness Index	5	5.6
Subindex A: Basic requirements	10	5.9
1st pillar: Institutions	22	5.2
2nd pillar: Infrastructure	8	6.1
3nd pillar: Macroeconomic environment	15	6.0
4th pillar: Health and primary education	14	6.5
Subindex B: Efficiency enhancers	7	5.4
5th pillar: Higher education and training	16	5.6
6th pillar: Goods market efficiency	23	5.0
7th pillar: Labor market efficiency	22	4.8
8th pillar: Financial market development	20	4.9
9th pillar: Technological readiness	10	6.1
10th pillar: Market size	5	6.0
Subindex C: Innovation and sophistication factors	3	5.6
11th pillar: Business sophistication	3	5.6
12th pillar: Innovation	5	5.6

Key Indicators, 2015

Population (millions)	81.9
GDP (US$ billions)	3357.6
GDP per capita (US$)	40996.5
GDP (PPP) % world GDP	3.38

Former Rankings

Edition	Rank	Score
2012-13	6 / 144	5.5
2013-14	4 / 148	5.5
2014-15	5 / 144	5.5
2015-16	4 / 140	5.5
2016-17	5 / 138	5.6

The Global Competitiveness Report 2016–2017, p. viii, 187

Who ? 138 different economies are analysed by the World Economic Forum.

What? Global Competitiveness Index: The Global Competitiveness Index (GCI) looks at contributing factors to a country's competiveness.

When? The index is published yearly in the form of the Global Competitiveness Report.

How? The GCI attempts to quantify the impact of a number of key factors which contribute to create the conditions for competitiveness, with particular focus on the macroeconomic environment, the quality of the country's institutions, and the state of the country's technology and supporting infrastructure.

Source: http://www.gaportal.org/global-indicators/global-competitiveness-index (12.5.2017)

Exercises

1. Put in order (most important – less important) the location factors for different types of businesses: automobile, textile, telecommunication services (M 10).
2. Explain the key information given in the text (M 11) and the graph (M 12) about Germany's global competiveness.
3. Evaluate Germany's industrial competitiveness from the perspective of an SME looking to move production of medical devices to Germany (M 10 – M 12) by writing a recommendation.
4. Discuss how Germany can best maintain its global competitiveness. Use the following terms: wages, taxes, innovation, education system, energy costs and infrastructure ...

2.4 The German Automotive Industry and Globalisation

M 13 German Automotive Industry: Key Trade Partners

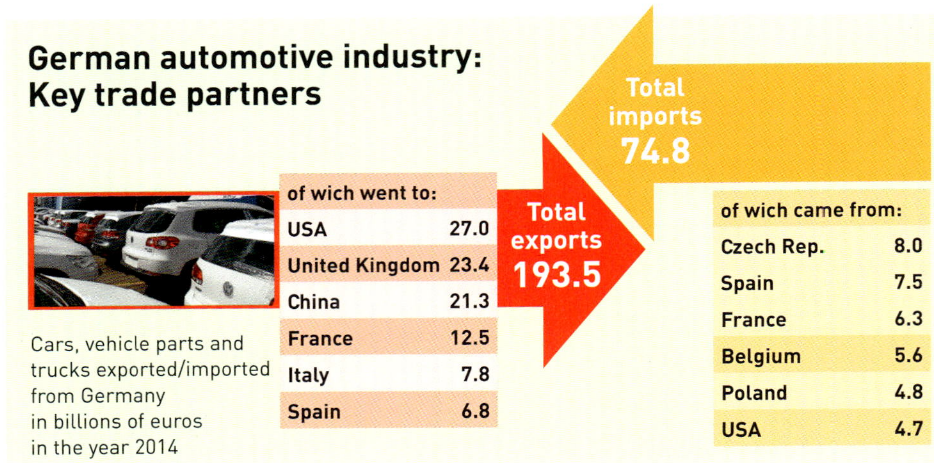

© 2015 IW Medien – iwd 39, Institut der deutschen Wirtschaft, Köln

M 14 "Made in Germany" no Longer Pride of German Carmakers?

"Made in Germany" was always the ultimate stamp of quality for iconic home-grown brands such as BMW, Audi and Mercedes, but is becoming increasingly obsolete as manufacturers ramp up production abroad. In fact, since 2010, more German cars are built outside the country than are assembled in domestic plants, even if their reputation for quality remains undiminished. The phenomenon "reflects the preference of manufacturers, and not just German ones, to produce more in the markets the cars are destined for," such as China or the United States, said Stefan Bratzel, director of the Center of Automotive Management at the University of Applied Sciences in Bergisch-Gladbach. It is also a way of "boosting their image because they can be seen by customers as generating employment in the specific regions," said Christoph Skudelny, automobile specialist at management consultants PwC. "But it's also a way of meeting certain demands by the governments of the countries concerned, as well as cutting logistic costs and exchange rate risks," Skudelny said. [...]

Furthermore, this has not been at the expense of Germany, where domestic production has also expanded, if not quite as fast, to 5.6 million units last year. The trend looks set to continue, too, VDA believes. It forecasts German makers will assemble some 8.7 million vehicle outside the country in 2013. That will take the proportion of overseas production up to 63 percent in 2013 from 60 percent in 2012. [...]

Luxury sports car maker Porsche is the sole exception, producing all of its cars in Germany. Daimler, which owns the famous Mercedes-Benz brand, expects to produce only half of its cars in Germany by the end of the decade compared with two thirds at present, a spokesman said. [...] And customers themselves do not seem overly con-

iconic home grown = here: famous local brands

undiminished = not decreasing or declining

VDA = Verband der Automobilindustrie

PwC = Pricewaterhouse-Coopers, a business consulting agency

Suppliers to the new BMW 3 series

Automotive News Europe

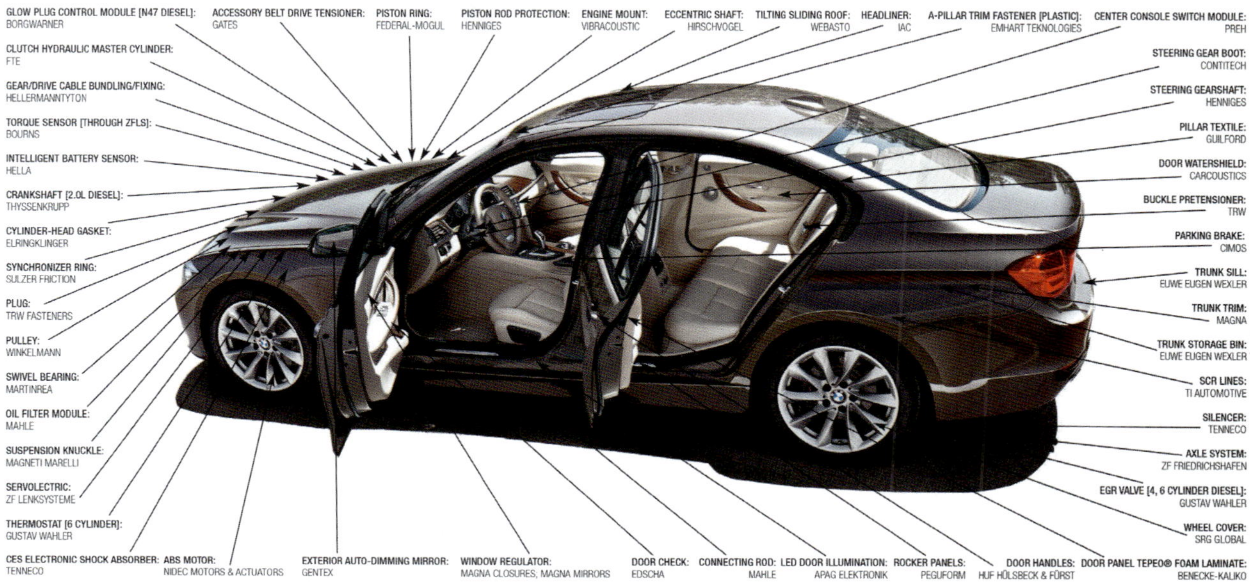

ILLUSTRATION: ANITA KAPOOR

cerned about where their cars are actually built. According to a study by Cetelem, only 5.0 percent of European car buyers attach any importance to that. Nevertheless, "the more upscale the model, the more the production location becomes important" for customers, Christoph Stuermer, analyst at IHS Automotive.

Manufacturers have cottoned on to this and now promote the merits of "developed in Germany" rather than "made in Germany".

"German engineering enjoys a good reputation. It's that which puts them ahead," said Juergen Pieper, analyst at Metzler. For the moment, the increased production abroad "has not only created jobs overseas but in Germany, too," where the sector employs 750,000 people, said VDA board member Klaus Braeunig.

esp / spm / asp ©Agence France-Press, 11 Sep 2013 (24.3.2017)

Cetelem = name of a bank group

IHS Automotive = automotive consulting agency

M 15 ● BMW to Build Next-Gen 3-Series sedan in Mexico Starting in 2019

SAN LUIS POTOSI, Mexico – BMW AG will revive North America output of its best-selling U.S. model when it begins producing the next-generation 3-series sedan in a new factory here starting in 2019.

BMW said it plans to build as many as 150,000 3-series cars, and possibly another vehicle, at the plant annually. The company is investing $1 billion to establish the plant, its second North American manufacturing hub. [...]

The company builds the 3-series sold in the U.S. now in Germany and South Africa, but South African output will cease when the Mexican plant comes online.

BMW joins other European manufacturers in building factories in Mexico to take advantage of low-cost labor, a growing supplier network and free-trade pacts. An estimated 70 percent of the vehicles to be produced at the Mexico plant will be sold in the NAFTA region, BMW officials say.

The company, according to media reports in Mexico, received $236 million in local

hub = here: center

aid in return for a commitment to create 1,500 jobs and invest $1 billion by 2024.
Under the deal, the automaker will not be required to pay state and local taxes for 10 years, Mexican economic development officials said Wednesday at a briefing.
BMW executives said the factory, on a 300-acre greenfield site, will take advantage of new sustainability technology to be environmentally friendly.
The plant will have its own body, paint and assembly shops, but engines and transmissions will be imported from Germany as they are for vehicles produced at BMW's Spartanburg, (South Carolina, USA) assembly plant. [...]
Personnel from BMW's Munich and Spartanburg plants will set up the Mexican factory. Employees from Munich, the lead factory for the 3-series sedan, will also train about 500 Mexican workers to be hired by 2019. [...]
By exporting from Mexico to Europe, BMW will avoid a 10 percent duty that it now pays on vehicles exported from the Spartanburg factory. [...] About 70 percent of the output at the Spartanburg plant is exported.

Diana T. Kurylko, Automotive News, 16 June 2016, http://www.autonews.com/apps/pbcs.dll/article?AID=/20160616/OEM01/160619925&template=print; (11.5.2017)

Exercises

1. Analyse the German automotive industry´s global interdependency (M 13, M 14).
2. Evaluate if a "German" car (BMW, Mercedes-Benz, Audi, etc.) made outside of Germany should still be considered "made in Germany" (M 14, M 15).
3. The BMW AG plans to move part of its luxury auto production to Mexico in order to save on costs and be closer to the countries it is exporting to. In groups of four discuss the advantages and disadvantages of moving production economically as well as how it affects the company's image (M 14, M 15). Present your results.

2.5 Who Profits From Globalisation?

M 16 ● Globalisation – Chance for Sub-Saharan Africa?

Passengers waiting for a train at a new station in Addis Ababa, 2015

The 32km light-rail project that had been under construction in Ethiopia's capital, Addis Ababa, finally opened [2015] becoming sub-Saharan Africa's first light-rail system. [...]
The system, which will expand next month to total 39 stations across the city, is expected to carry 15,000 people per hour in one direction. The much-anticipated infrastructure project was built over three years by a Chinese company after the Ethiopian government secured 85% of funding from the Export-Import Bank of China. Meanwhile, a much-delayed light-rail system in Lagos is still under construction.

Francesca Perry, The Guardian, 25 Sep 2015 (12.4.2017)

M 17 ● Winners and Losers in Globalisation by Countries

Globalisation has made the world a better and more equal place for many more people than was the case a few decades ago. However, it has also created two well-defined worlds of poor countries and wealthy nations, according to Vanesa Jordá and José María Sarabia of the University of Cantabria in Spain. In an article [...] they studied the distribution of well-being over the last wave of globalisation between 1980 and 2011.
Well-being is generally described as the state of being happy, healthy or prosperous. The researchers used the UN Human Development Index as an indicator of quality of life. It offers a realistic perspective of the

national levels of well-being of 130 countries, covering almost 90 percent of the world's population. The Index also takes into account non-income dimensions such as education and health.

HDI Report 2016

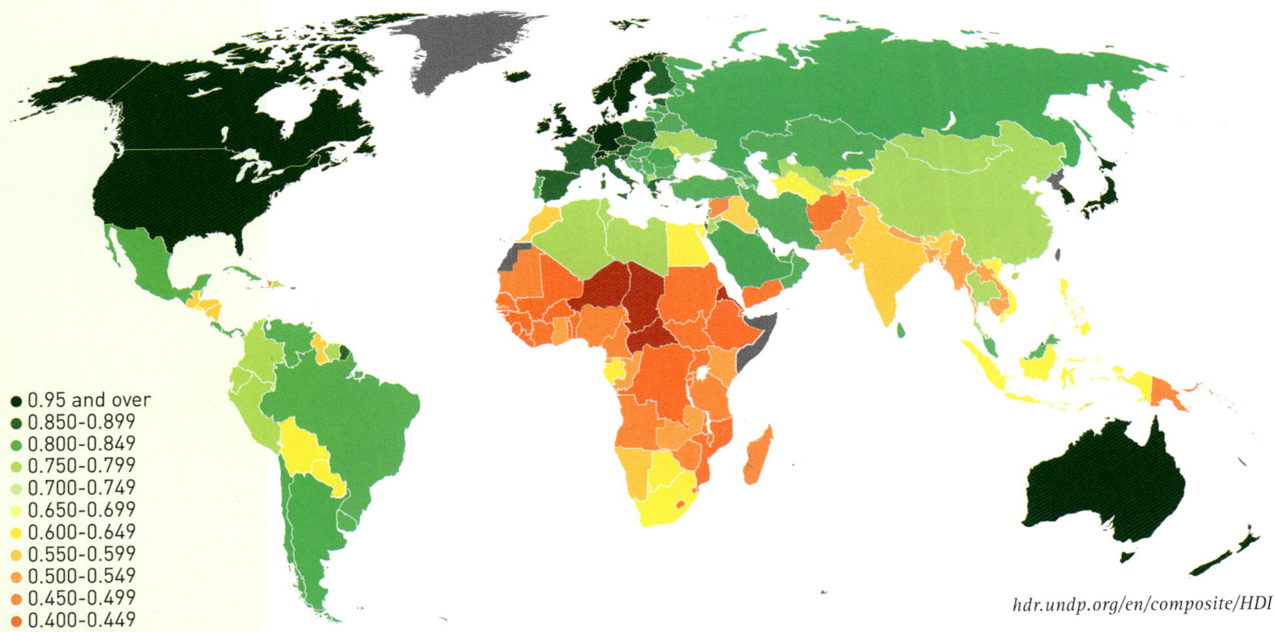

hdr.undp.org/en/composite/HDI

It shows that globalisation has brought higher levels of development to more countries than was the case 30 years ago. However, the intensity by which well-being has increased differs across countries. This has created two well-defined clusters: one of least developed countries in especially Sub-Saharan Africa, and another of highly developed countries. At the same time, medium developed nations, such as China and India, have caught up with the advanced economies. [...]

The greatest decrease in disparities was found in education, which presents reductions of up to 64 percent. This is thanks to enhanced efforts towards education in developing countries over the last 40 years, especially in Asia. It is consistent with the belief that globalisation promotes investment in education and helps countries to develop.

On the health side, no real catch-up or convergence was seen during the nineties. However, this is changing over the past ten years thanks to the expansion of health technology and medicines. [...]

"The benefits of globalisation have increased a number of aspects of well-being in most countries. However, these advantages have not reached a group of countries which are not able to overcome the human development barriers in health and income. They are being trapped in a low pole which shows little sign of their catching up or converging to the general trend," conclude Jordá and Sarabia.

V. Jordá / J.h. Sarabia, Winners and losers of globalization by countries, 2014

M 18 Global Income Dynamics

Globalisation has radically changed global income dynamics. So who has won and who has lost?

It is generally thought that two groups are the big winners of the past two decades of globalisation: the very rich (those at the top of national and global income distributions) and the middle classes of emerging market economies, especially in China, India, Indonesia and Brazil.

These results [of a database of the World Bank] give us a much more nuanced picture of the effects of the recent two decades of globalisation. Who gained and who lost? Specifically, which parts of the global income distribution registered the largest gains between 1988 and 2008?

As the figure below shows, most significant increases in per capita income are indeed found among the very top of the global income distribution and among the emerging global middle class, which includes more than a third of the world's population. [...]

The top 1 % of the global income distribution has seen its real income (adjusted for inflation) rise by more than 60 % over those two decades.

[...] The real surprise is that those in the bottom third of the global income distribution have also made significant gains, with real incomes rising between more than 40 % and almost 70 %. (The only exception is the poorest 5 % of the population, whose real incomes have remained about the same.)

It is precisely this income increase in the bottom of the global pyramid that has allowed the proportion of what the World Bank calls the absolute poor (people whose per capita income is less than 1.25 PPP dollars per day) to decrease from 44 % to 23 % over approximately the same 20 years.

But the biggest losers of globalisation – or at least the "non-winners" (other than the very poorest 5 %) – were those between the 75th and 90th percentile of the global income distribution. Their real income gains were essentially nil. These people represent what can be called a global upper-middle class. Their ranks include the citizens of rich countries with stagnant real incomes as well as many people from former Communist countries and Latin America.

Branko Milanovic, 25 Oct 2012, http://www.theglobalist.com/the-real-winners-and-losers-of-globalisation/, (12.5.2017)

nuanced = here: detailed

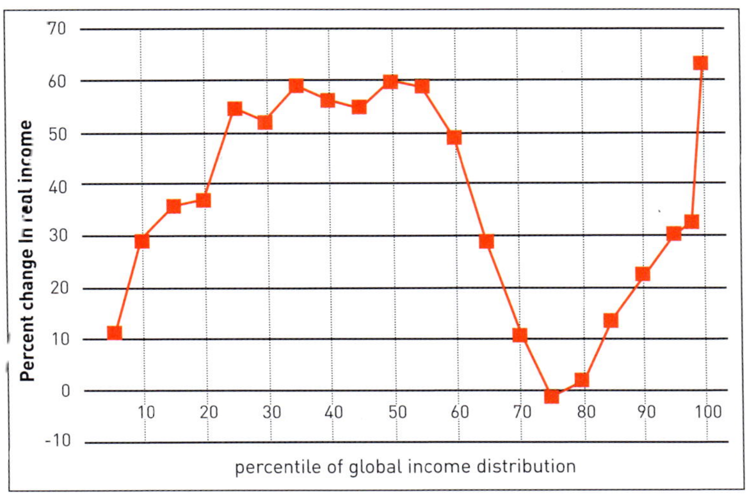

Percentage change in real income between 1988 and 2008 at various percentiles of global income distribution (in 2005 PPP dollars). Data source: World Bank.

M 19 How is the Industry Coping with Globalisation?

Over the past few decades, there has been a shift in economic power from the established, industralised countries to the emerging, industrialising countries. While the established countries still accounted for 81.4 percent of the global economy in 1995, their share had dropped to 63.5 percent by 2012. The importance of the emerging, industrialising countries has grown; their share of the global economy increased from 12.8 to 27.8 percent between 1995 and 2012. This shift is particularly evident in the industrial sector, where new economic power centres have seen their share of value added rise from 16.2 to 41.3 percent, much of that at the expense of the established countries. Most notably, China's share grew to 24.4 percent.

In the sphere of international trade, the rising competitors increased their share of global exports from 14.3 to 25.1 percent. As for the established, industrialised countries, while their percentage of the pie has declined, they have benefited from the growth triggered by the emerging, industrialising countries.

Germany has lost some of its share of the global market to new competitors over the past 20 years. In the global industrial sector, its share of value added dropped roughly from nine to six percent between 1995 and 2012. In absolute terms, however, Germany was able to increase its industrial value added by 45 percent between 1995 and 2013, from 338.1 to 561.3 billion euros. Germany is clearly one of globalisation's winners. Few established, industrialised countries have had comparable success at turning globalisation to their advantage. Between 1995 and 2012, industrial value added grew by only three percent in France and nine percent in the United Kingdom. In Japan, it dropped by seven percent. Germany has been able to maintain its share of the global export market – benefiting from dynamic market trends in the new competitor countries; close international ties, particularly within the European production network; and integration into international value chains.

Germany has significant strengths relative to other countries, but one of its weaknesses is costs. A strong emphasis on technology

international value chains = the different processes in different parts of the world that each add value to the goods or services being produced

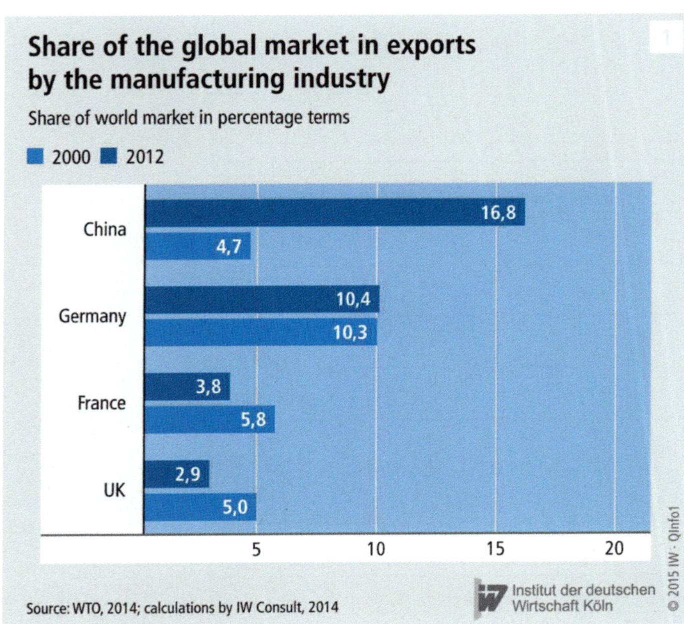

has allowed German industry to gain a temporary advantage, but it is under increasing pressure. Two-thirds of industrial firms believe that Chinese competitors will have made great strides in narrowing the technological gap within the next five years. Furthermore, one-third of companies with foreign production sites indicate that their foreign activities are replacing domestic production. All of this suggests that the pace at which Germany is losing ground as an industrial site is accelerating somewhat.

Agnes Millack, 30.5.2015, https://www.iwkoeln.de/en/press/iwd/beitrag/german-firms-how-is-the-industry-coping-with-globalisation-217506, (12.5.2017)

strides = advances in a certain area

Exercises

1. Discuss whether or not construction of the light rail system in Addis Ababa would have been possible without globalisation (M 16).
2. Comment on the quote, "The benefits of globalisation have increased a number of aspects of well-being in most countries" (M 17).
3. Create a table for the "winners" and "losers" of globalisation and assign information from M 18 to each column.
4. Explain whether Germany can be considered a global "winner" or "loser" (M 18 – M 19).

3. How Can Global Institutions Help Solve Global Problems?

3.1 How to Deal with a Financial Crisis in a Globalised World?

M 1 What Pushed Greece to Financial Aid?

Cartoon: Amorim/Cartoon Movement

Greece became the center of Europe's debt crisis after the New York Stock Exchange also known as "Wall Street" nearly crashed in 2008. This sent the global financial markets into chaos which resulted in Greece announcing in October 2009 that it had been inaccurately stating its deficit figures for years, raising alarms about the overall health of Greek finances. As a result Greece was no longer able to borrow within the financial markets. By the spring of 2010, it was headed towards bankruptcy, which threatened to start a new financial crisis.

inaccurately stating its deficit figures = giving false numbers on how much money is owed

To avoid a complete disaster, the International Monetary Fund, the European Central Bank and the European Commission issued the first of two international bailouts for Greece which would eventually total to more than € 240 billion.

However, the bailout came with conditions. Lenders set up harsh austerity terms which meant big budget cuts and large tax increases. They also required Greece to fix its economy by cutting lots of government positions, ending people's ability to avoid taxes, and making Greece an easier place to do business.

Why is there still a crisis if Greece has received billions of Euros in bailouts?

The plan was that the money would "buy" Greece some time to fix its finances and calm market fears that the euro union could break up. Although this has helped in some aspects, in the past five years the economy has shrunk by 25 % and unemployment is also about 25 %.

The bailout money has mainly gone towards paying off Greece's international loans, rather than helping the economy. And the government still has a lot of debt that cannot be paid off unless the economy starts to recover and continues to recover.

Greece's relationships to Europe are in a fragile state, and several of its leaders are becoming impatient and unlikely to tolerate the slow progress that has often occurred in the past. Under the bailout agreement, Greece must continue to reform many of its systems, many of which should have been put in place years ago.

M 2 What is the IMF?

The IMF, also known as the Fund, was conceived at a UN conference in Bretton Woods, New Hampshire, United States, in July 1944. The 44 countries at that conference sought to build a framework for economic cooperation to avoid a repetition of the competitive devaluations that had contributed to the Great Depression of the 1930s.

Responsibilities: The IMF's primary purpose is to ensure the stability of the international monetary system – the system of exchange rates and international payments that enables countries (and their citizens) to transact with each other. The Fund's mandate was updated in 2012 to include all macroeconomic and financial sector issues that bear on global stability.

Fundamental Mission: The IMF's fundamental mission is to ensure the stability of the international monetary system. It does so in three ways: keeping track of the global economy and the economies of member countries; lending to countries with balance of payments difficulties; and giving practical help to members.

Surveillance: The IMF oversees the international monetary system and monitors the economic and financial policies of its 189 member countries. As part of this process, which takes place both at the global level and in individual countries, the IMF highlights possible risks to stability and advises on needed policy adjustments.

Lending: A core responsibility of the IMF is to provide loans to member countries experiencing actual or potential balance of payments problems. This financial assistance enables countries to rebuild their international reserves, stabilise their currencies, continue paying for imports, and restore conditions for strong economic growth, while undertaking policies to correct underlying problems. Unlike development banks, the IMF does not lend for specific projects.

Capacity Development: IMF capacity development – technical assistance and training – helps member countries design and implement economic policies that foster stability and growth by strengthening their institutional capacity and skills. [...] The IMF has a management team and 17 departments that carry out its country, policy, analytical, and technical work. [...]

Management: The IMF has a Managing Director, who is head of the staff and Chairperson of the Executive Board. The Managing Director is appointed by the Executive Board for a renewable term of five years and is assisted by a First Deputy Managing Director and three Deputy Managing Directors.

Staff: The IMF's employees come from all over the world; they are responsible to the IMF and not to the authorities of the countries of which they are citizens.

IMF resources: Most resources for IMF loans are provided by member countries, primarily through their payment of quotas.

Quotas: Quota subscriptions are a central component of the IMF's financial resources. Each member country of the IMF is assigned a quota, based broadly on its relative position in the world economy. [...]

Country Representation: Unlike the General Assembly of the United Nations, where each country has one vote, decision making at the IMF was designed to reflect the relative positions of its member countries in the global economy. [...]

Accountability: Created in 1945, the IMF is governed by and accountable to the 189 countries that make up its near-global membership. [...]

http://www.imf.org/external/about.htm (12.4.2017)

conceived = created

devaluations = decreasing the worth of a country's currency in comparison to other currencies

implement = put in place
foster = make a good environment for

component = part

M 3 IMF Survey: Grounds for Cautious Optimism in Greece

Speaking to IMF Survey, Poul Thomsen, head of the IMF's Greece team answers questions on the future of Greece.

IMF Survey: How do you see economic prospects and what are the key challenges ahead?

Thomsen: First, let's remember where we were not long ago. Back in mid-2012, when the current government coalition took office, there were widespread doubts about Greece's future in the euro zone. The government's determined policy actions since then have taken "Grexit" off the table, and we are now seeing signs of economic stabilisation. The contraction of the economy slowed further in the first quarter of 2014 to - 0.9 percent year-on-year, and the unemployment rate has declined slightly in recent months. The government re-accessed markets for the first time since the crisis, and with rising investor interest, market access for Greek banks and corporates is also improving faster than anticipated. Overall, these developments suggest grounds for cautious optimism, and we expect growth to turn positive in 2014, for the first time since 2007.

It is too early to declare victory though, as policies need to build on what has been achieved, to improve confidence further and lay the ground for the recovery to turn into sustained and robust growth. [...]

IMF Survey: What is your view on the need for further debt relief?

Thomsen: There is an agreed framework in place for ensuring debt sustainability, with Greece's European partners agreeing to provide any additional debt relief as needed to help bring Greece's debt down to 124 percent of GDP by 2020 and to substantially below 110 percent of GDP by 2022, as long as Greece continues to deliver on its program commitments. With Greece now having achieved a fiscal primary surplus, these issues are likely to be discussed with the European partners in the context of the forthcoming program review.

https://www.imf.org/external/pubs/ft/survey/so/2014/car060914a.htm, 10.6.2014 (13.5.2017)

sustained and robust growth = economic growth that continues and can be maintained despite market changes

determined = focused

contraction of the economy = when the economy as a whole is in decline

M 4 Greece's Debt Costs Rise Sharply as Worries Grow over IMF Role

The renewed focus on Greece's debts came as the International Monetary Fund revealed its board was split over how far spending cuts in the country should go, raising fresh doubts over its participation in rescue plans for the struggling Greek economy.

The Washington-based fund has made repeated warnings that Greece's debt burden of about €330bn (£280bn) is unsustainable despite the government pushing through spending cuts and tax increases that have badly hit popularity ratings for the government of prime minister Alexis Tsipras.

The IMF declined to join other international lenders – the European Central Bank and the European Union – in funding the country's third bailout, agreed in August 2015, and it is currently deciding whether to take part in a new chunk of rescue funds needed by mid-2018. Germany has warned the IMF's involvement is crucial if support for Greece is to continue.

News of a split on the IMF board raised new questions over whether Germany will see its wish granted for the fund joining the next rescue. In its latest annual review of the Greek economy, the IMF revealed that its board members were in disagreement over whether Athens should enforce even more austerity to satisfy its lenders.

Most of the 24-strong group agreed that

crucial = very important

unsustainable = unable to be maintained

austerity = policies that try to decrease government budget deficits, this is often done through spending cuts, tax increases or both

Greece was on track to achieve a primary surplus of 1.5 % of GDP, and should not make further cuts. However, another group on the board argued that Athens needed to tighten further to push its surplus up to 3.5 % of GDP, the level agreed in its last bailout. A primary surplus refers to a government's income exceeding its spending, excluding debt interest payments.

In a rare admission of an internal split, the IMF said: "Most executive directors agreed with the thrust of the staff appraisal while some directors had different views on the fiscal path and debt sustainability."[...]

Dijsselbloem also said that Greece's creditors would still be prepared to ease terms of Greece's debt further, if the country continues to cooperate on reforms. But he ruled out the prospect of Greek debt being forgiven, or cancelled altogether.

The Greek government, which faces more debt repayment deadlines this summer [2017], said it was hoping for a "positive conclusion" to the protracted review of its bailout programme. A resolution would help unlock disbursements from the latest bailout that are needed to pay for these debt repayments but may also open the way for Greece's bonds to be included in the European Central Bank's bond-buying programme, a development that in turn would likely lower Greece's high borrowing costs.

But Greek government spokesman Dimitris Tzanakopoulos also insisted Athens was not about to yield to demands for it to implement more austerity after the bailout scheme ends in 2018.

"The government's position is clear and it has been expressed categorically ... Our aim is to not yield to illogical demands by the International Monetary Fund, which insists on legislating precautionary (austerity) measures after the programme ends," he said.

Katie Allen and Graeme Wearden, The Guardian, 7 Feb 2017 (13.9.2017)

protracted = lengthy, delayed

disbursements = payment of money

thrust = principal direction

appraisal = evaluation

Exercises

1. Analyse the cartoon in M 1.
2. Comment on the title question in M 1, "What pushed Greece to financial aid?" Be sure to address the chain of events and main actors. Add information from background knowledge you have of the crisis.
3. Create a diagram that shows the functions and responsibilities of the IMF (M 2).
4. Explain the role of the IMF in the Greek financial crisis through the lens of the IMF's goals and responsibilities (M 3, M 4).
5. Has the IMF positively or negatively affected the financial crisis in Greece? Evaluate this question and justify your opinion with information from M 1 - M 4.

3.2 Why Do Countries Need Loans from Global Institutions?

M 5 ● Millennium Development Goals and Africa

Cartoon: Chappatte/International Herald Tribune, 24.9.2010

M 6 ● Millennium Development Goals

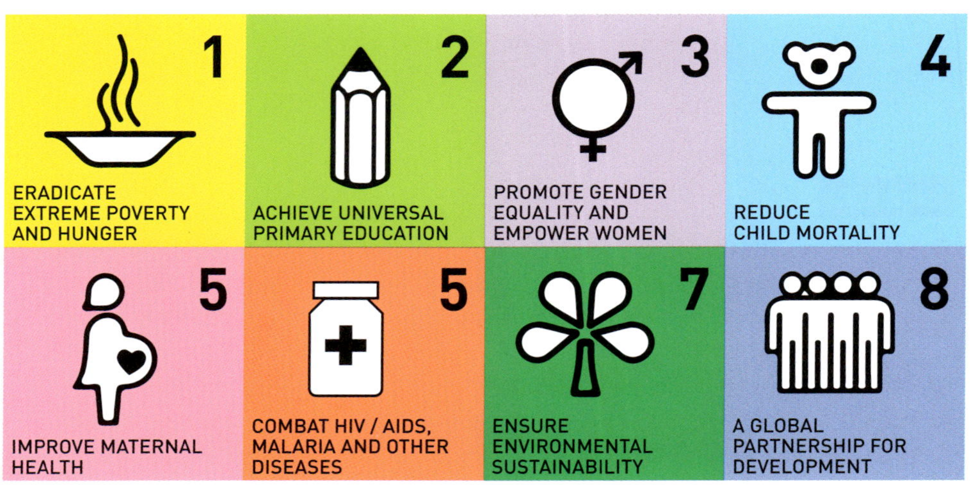

UNDP Brazil

In September 2000 world leaders came together at United Nations Headquarters in New York to adopt the United Nations Millennium Declaration, committing their nations to a new global partnership to reduce extreme poverty and setting out a series of time-bound targets - with a deadline of 2015 - that have become known as the Millenni-um Development Goals.

M 7 Millennium Development Goals´ Outcomes 2015

- Globally, the number of those living in extreme poverty declined by more than half, falling from 1.9 billion in 1990 to 836 million in 2015, with most progress occurring since 2000.
- Net primary school enrolment in developing regions has reached 91 per cent, up from 83 per cent in 2000.
- Many more girls are now in school compared to 2000, with developing regions as a whole achieving the target to eliminate gender disparity in primary, secondary and tertiary education.
- Global under-five mortality has declined by more than half, dropping from 90 to 43 deaths per 1,000 live births between 1990 and 2015, from 12.7 million in 1990 to almost six million despite population growth in developing regions.
- Maternal mortality has declined by 45 percent worldwide since 1990, with most of the reduction occurring since 2000.
- New HIV infections fell by approximately 40 per cent between 2000 and 2013 from an estimated 3.5 million cases to 2.1 million […]
- Official development aid from developed countries grew by 66 per cent in real terms between 2000 and 2014.

But progress has been uneven across regions and countries, leaving millions of people behind, especially the poorest and those disadvantaged due to sex, age, disability, ethnicity or geographic location.

http://www.un.org/milleniumgoals/bhgd.shtml, 12/2015 (17.9.2017)

M 8 How Does the World Bank Help Developing Countries?

The World Bank Group (WBG) started in 1944 as the International Bank for Reconstruction and Development (IBRD). Its main goal was to restore post-WWII Europe. Over 75 years later the World Bank is an international organisation primarily concerned with combating poverty through developmental assistance in low and middle income countries. Some specific examples of developmental assistance are loans, technological support and assistance, training and giving advice on policy in both the public and private sectors.

Membership to the IBRD has certain requirements, but it is not exclusive. Today there are 184 member countries or shareholders at the IBRD, which is one of the World Bank's most important institutions. In order to become a shareholder a country has to join the International Monetary Fund (IMF). The number of shareholders a member is allowed to have is based on the country's economy.

restore = to help rebuild

combating = here: working to eliminate

The World Bank Group consists of five organisations. The International Bank for Reconstruction and Development (IBRD) lends to governments of middle-income and creditworthy low-income countries. The International Development Association (IDA) provides interest-free loans — called credits — and grants to governments of the poorest countries. Together, IBRD and IDA make up the World Bank.

acquiring = gaining

burdensome = difficult

The President of the World Bank is selected from the largest shareholder, which is currently the United States. The Board of Governors represents members. Specific powers are given to a board of 24 executive directors. Nineteen executive directors represent the member states as heads of smaller state groups, while the five largest economies or shareholders each have their own executive director. The five largest shareholders are currently the U.S., U.K., France, Germany and Japan. The World Bank is funded by wealthy countries and from its sale of bonds in global capital markets.

This funding is then used to help nations build and rebuild themselves. During this process they sometimes need more aid than planned to overcome hurdles economically and socially. This has often led to countries acquiring more debt than they can handle, making payments burdensome. To avoid this, each of the bank's customers is advised to create and implement policies that encourage not only economic growth and reform, but growth in other areas such as health, education, the environment, limiting poverty as well as promoting small businesses.

M 9 Demand for World Bank Lending on the Rise as Countries Face Headwinds

economic headwinds = an economic situation that makes growth more difficult

deteriorated = to become worse

eclipse = be higher than the year before

As developing countries continue to face strong economic headwinds, demand for lending from the World Bank has risen to levels never seen outside a financial crisis, and is on track to climb to more than $150 billion in support between the fiscal year 2013 and the current fiscal year.

"We are in a global economy where growth is expected to remain weak, so it is critically important that the World Bank play our traditional role of helping developing countries accelerate growth," said World Bank Group President Jim Yong Kim. "We have an historic opportunity to end extreme poverty in the world by 2030 but the only way we can achieve this goal is if developing countries – from middle-income to low-income nations – get back on the path of faster growth that helps the poorest and most vulnerable."

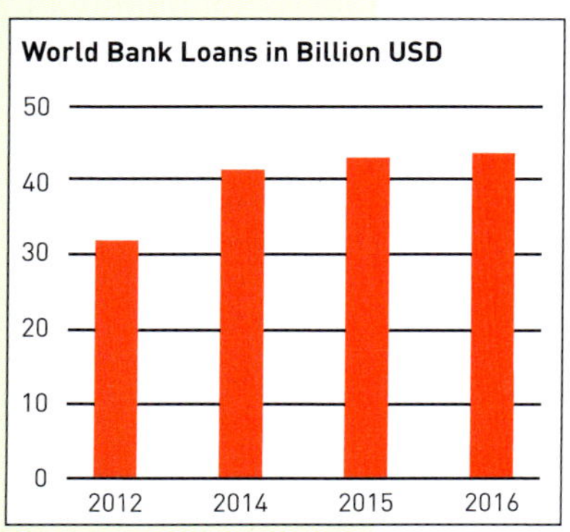

Global economic growth is projected at 2.9 percent in 2016, picking up at a slower pace than previously expected from an estimated 2.4 percent in 2015. However, conditions have generally deteriorated further since the start of the year. In the face of these challenges, demand from middle-income countries for IBRD lending in our last fiscal year, 2015, was the highest it has ever been outside a financial crisis at $23.5 billion. The Bank expects that 2016 will easily eclipse that record, with lending projected to rise above $25 billion.

"Developing country governments are feeling the pressure to find additional ways to accelerate growth, in the current downturn," said Jan Walliser, Vice President for Equitable Growth, Finance, and Institutions. "Improving long-term growth trends now calls for a broad set of legal, regulatory, institutional, and even logistical reforms that make investing more attractive. Focusing now on structural reform is the recommendation of both mainstream economists and of G20 governments."

The World Bank Group has longstanding experience in advising on and supporting implementation of country-driven reforms. The Bank offers a unique mix of deep country knowledge, sectoral expertise, and distilled global experience.

World Bank, Press Release, April 11, 2016, http://www.worldbank.org/en/news/press-release/2016/04/11/demand-world-bank-lending-countries-headwinds (7.6.2017)

M 10 Opposition to the Bank

Dams, power plants, conservation programs and other projects financed by the World Bank have pushed an estimated 3.4 million people out of their homes, off their lands, or threatened their livelihoods, according to research by the International Consortium of Investigative Journalists and other media organizations published on Thursday. [...] Human rights organizations have long criticized the bank for failing to monitor the effects on communities of the programs it sponsors. [...] The World Bank admitted to "serious shortcomings in the implementation of its resettlement policies" after it had ordered an internal review of its actions. [...] However, identifying these shortcomings is not enough, says Jessica Evans, senior researcher and advocate for international financial institutions with Human Rights Watch (HRW). "After the World Bank has done its own review, it hasn't gone back and worked to identify these people. And find out how they were harmed and work for these people to properly remedy the harm," she told DW. [...] "The bank does not really verify the information that has been provided by the borrower. And obviously, the borrower has an economic advantage of not presenting the potential problems and the potential negative impact on communities because they want to get the loan. The bank is pushing this loan out the door in a much more rushed way." [...]

Poor people are most vulnerable to activities funded by the World Bank - the very same people the institution is trying to lift out of poverty. "People who are resettled often lose many of their livelihood opportunities. For instance, if they rely on subsistence agriculture, sometimes it takes some time to rebuild that agriculture in a new place. This is something that takes a significant amount of time to monitor and the [World] Bank needs to really invest in that," Evans said. [...]

Meanwhile, the World Bank has come up with a plan to reform its policies. "We must and will do better," a spokesperson told DW in a statement. However, human rights activists remain skeptical.

Sarah Steffen, 16 Apr 2015, http://www.dw.com/en/world-bank-failed-to-protect-the-poor-research-shows/a-18388491 (12.9.2017)

resettlement policies = policies to help people find new homes

subsistence agriculture = where farmers grow enough food for them and their families

Exercises

1. a) Analyse the cartoon in M 5.
   b) Discuss in class how loans for African countries and the Millennium Development Goals are tied together (M 5 – M 7).
2. Describe the functions and purposes of the World Bank (M 8).
3. Comment on why countries are not only applying for loans, but also using the World Bank's advisory services. What are the advantages and disadvantages of this approach (M 9)?
4. Explain why there is opposition to the World Bank (M 10).
5. Discuss with a partner how the role of the World Bank is a contributing factor in achieving the Millennium Development Goals.

3.3 How Does the WTO Resolve Trade Conflicts Between States?

M 11 Evolution of Chinese Rare Earth Elements Export Quotas

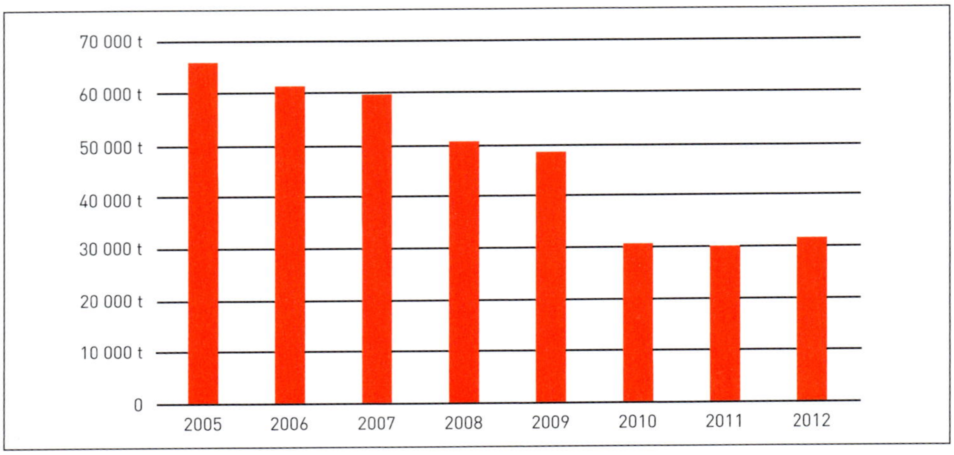

Data source: US Congress research service, March 2012

M 12 China – Measures Related to the Exportation of Various Raw Materials

Short title:	**China – Raw Materials**
Complainant:	Mexico
Respondent:	China
Third Parties:	Argentina; Brazil; Canada; Chile; Colombia; Ecuador; European Union; India; Japan; Korea, Republic of; Norway; Chinese Taipei; Turkey; Saudi Arabia, Kingdom of; United States
Agreements cited: (as cited in request for consultations)	GATT 1994: Art. VIII, VIII:1, VIII:4, X, X:1, X:3, XI, XI:1 Protocol of Accession: Part I, para. 1.2, Part I, para. 5.1, Part I, para. 5.2, Part I, para. 8.2, Part I, para. 11.3,
Request for Consultations received:	21 August 2009
Panel Report circulated:	5 July 2011
Appellate Body Report circulated:	30 January 2012

M 13 Trade Dispute Between China and Mexico

On 21 August 2009, Mexico requested consultations with China with respect to China's restraints on the export from China of various forms of raw materials. Mexico cites 32 measures through which China allegedly imposes restraints on the exports in question and note that there appear to be additional unpublished restrictive measures. [...] Mexico considers that the measures also appear to nullify or impair the benefits accruing to Mexico directly or indirectly under the cited agreements.
On 28 August 2009, the European Communities and the United States requested to join the consultations. On 4 September 2009, Colombia requested to join the consultations. On 7 September 2009, Canada requested to join the consultations. On 4 November 2009, Mexico requested the establishment of a panel. At its meeting on 19 November 2009, the DSB deferred the establishment of a panel.

Info

DSB – Dispute Settlement Body

The General Council convenes as the Dispute Settlement Body (DSB) to deal with disputes between WTO members. [...] The DSB has authority to establish dispute settlement panels, refer matters to arbitration, adopt panel, Appellate Body and arbitration reports, maintain surveillance over the implementation of recommendations and rulings contained in such reports, and authorize suspension of concessions in the event of non-compliance with those recommendations and rulings.

© World Trade Organization (WTO) 2017, https://www.wto.org/english/tratop_e/dispu_e/dispu_body_e.htm (7.6.2017)

consultations = a discussion between countries to find a solution before taking legal action

allegedly imposes restraints = being accused of putting limitations on something

disputes = disagreements

arbitration = the process of helping parties solve an argument by finding a solution

to defer = to delay s.th.

M 14 Understanding the WTO: Settling Disputes

Disputes in the WTO are essentially about broken promises. WTO members have agreed that if they believe fellow-members are violating trade rules, they will use the multilateral system of settling disputes instead of taking action unilaterally. That means abiding by the agreed procedures, and respecting judgements.
A dispute arises when one country adopts a trade policy measure or takes some action that one or more fellow-WTO members considers to be breaking the WTO agreements, or to be a failure to live up to obligations. A third group of countries can declare that they have an interest in the case and enjoy some rights. [...]
The Uruguay Round agreement introduced a more structured process with more clearly defined stages in the procedure. It introduced greater discipline for the length of time a case should take to be settled, with flexible deadlines set in various stages of the procedure. The agreement emphasizes that prompt settlement is essential if the WTO is to function effectively. It sets out in considerable detail the procedures and the timetable to be followed in resolving disputes. If a case runs its full course to a first ruling, it should not normally take more than about one year to 15 months if the case is appealed. The agreed time limits are flexible, and if the case is considered urgent (e.g. if perishable goods are involved), it is accelerated as much as possible.
The Uruguay Round agreement also made it impossible for the country losing a case to block the adoption of the ruling. Under the previous GATT procedure, rulings could only be adopted by consensus, meaning that a single objection could block the ruling. Now, rulings are automatically adopted unless there is a consensus to reject a

prompt = being completed without delay

unilaterally = actions taken by one group or country without the agreement or participation of others

resolving = to settle or solve

appeal = a formal question that asks about the correctness of the decision or ruling

adversary = opponent

resemble = look like

rebuttal = formal response to an accusation

sentiments = thoughts, feelings, or attitudes

remedy = the legal means of putting a "right" into action or correcting a "wrong"

ruling - any country wanting to block a ruling has to persuade all other WTO members (including its adversary in the case) to share its view.

Although much of the procedure does resemble a court or tribunal, the preferred solution is for the countries concerned to discuss their problems and settle the dispute by themselves. The first stage is therefore consultations between the governments concerned, and even when the case has progressed to other stages, consultation and mediation are still always possible. [...]

The case has been decided: what next?

Go directly to jail. Do not pass Go, do not collect ... . Well, not exactly. But the sentiments apply. If a country has done something wrong, it should swiftly correct its fault. And if it continues to break an agreement, it should offer compensation or face a suitable response that has some bite – although this is not actually a punishment: it's a "remedy", the ultimate goal being for the country to comply with the ruling.

The priority is for the losing "defendant" to bring its policy into line with the ruling or recommendations, and it is given time to do this. The dispute settlement agreement stresses that "prompt compliance with recommendations or rulings of the DSB [Dispute Settlement Body] is essential in order to ensure effective resolution of disputes to the benefit of all Members".

© World Trade Organization (WTO) 2017, https://www.wto.org/english/thewto_e/whatis_e/tif_e/disp1_e.htm (5.7.2017)

Info

How Does a Panel Work?

Before the first hearing:
each side in the dispute presents its case in writing to the panel.

First hearing: the case for the complaining country and defence:
the complaining country (or countries), the responding country, and those that have announced they have an interest in the dispute, make their case at the panel's first hearing.

Rebuttals:
the countries involved submit written rebuttals and present oral arguments at the panel's second meeting.

Experts:
if one side raises scientific or other technical matters, the panel may consult experts or appoint an expert review group to prepare an advisory report.

First draft:
the panel submits the descriptive (factual and argument) sections of its report to the two sides, giving them two weeks to comment. This report does not include findings and conclusions.

Interim report:
The panel then submits an interim report, including its findings and conclusions, to the two sides, giving them one week to ask for a review.

Review:
The period of review must not exceed two weeks. During that time, the panel may hold additional meetings with the two sides.

Final report:
A final report is submitted to the two sides and three weeks later, it is circulated to all WTO members. If the panel decides that the disputed trade measure does break a WTO agreement or an obligation, it recommends that the measure be made to conform with WTO rules. The panel may suggest how this could be done.

The report becomes a ruling:
The report becomes the Dispute Settlement Body's ruling or recommendation within 60 days unless a consensus rejects it. Both sides can appeal the report (and in some cases both sides do).

M 15 The EU in the Trade Dispute

Both the European Commission and EU ministers have supported plans to ensure that industries get better access to raw materials, as competition for access to commodities such as rare metals becomes fiercer with globalisation.

Of particular concern to Europeans are Rare Earth Elements (REE), a series of metals and elements used to manufacture high-tech products such as wind turbines, electronic consumer goods, nanotechnologies, batteries for electric cars and various military applications.

According to the EU, China is the largest provider of rare earths, with 97 % of world production. But since 2005 it has dramatically reduced export quotas on a number of rare metals (down from 60,000 tons in 2006 to 14,500 tons in 2011) and is mulling a full export ban as of 2015.

In a joint effort with the United States and Mexico, the EU took action against China in June 2009, initiating a WTO dispute settlement case for restricting exports of industrial raw materials.

Euractiv, 1 Sept 2011, https://www.euractiv.com/section/sustainable-dev/news/china-appeals-raw-materials-wto-case/ (5.6.2017)

mulling = thinking about

fiercer = here: intense

initiating = starting

M 16 China Appeals Raw Materials WTO Case

China has appealed a World Trade Organisation ruling against its export policies on raw materials, the Ministry of Commerce said, in a move which could have implications for its rare earth exports.

The decision, posted to the ministry's website late on Wednesday (31 August 2011), made good on its promise to appeal the case before the trade body's 2 September 2011 deadline.

In July, a WTO legal panel dismissed China's claim that its system of export duties and quotas on raw materials – used in the production of steel, electronics and medicines – served to protect its environment and scarce resources.

The WTO's July ruling applies to elements including bauxite, coking coal, fluorspar, magnesium, manganese, silicon metal, silicon carbide, yellow phosphorus and zinc, all key industrial materials.

That ruling was a victory for the United States, the European Union and Mexico, which took China to the WTO in 2009, saying export restrictions on these raw materials discriminated against foreign manufacturers and gave an unfair advantage to domestic producers.

The decision was also seen as a potential precedent against China's stance on its exports of 17 rare earth minerals, of which China produces about 97 % of the world's supplies.

China has cut exports of rare earths to the dismay of importers, which use the minerals in producing high-tech products and defence applications. The WTO appellate body is required to make a decision within three months of China's appeal.

Euractiv, 1 Sept 2011, https://www.euractiv.com/section/sustainable-dev/news/china-appeals-raw-materials-wto-case/ (14.7.2017)

implications = effects or consequences in the future

precedent = a case that serves as a guide for similar situations in the future

stance = attitude, approach

M 17 EU Wins WTO Battle Against China over Raw Materials

level playing field = where everyone has equal chances to compete

abide = accept or agree to the ruling

launched = started

choking off global supplies = to suddenly stop the movement or access of supplies to others

accession = the process of joining

barred = prevented

substantial = a good or considerable amount of something

tremendous = something extraordinary or excellent

China lost an appeal at the World Trade Organisation on Monday (30 January 2012) in a case about its export restrictions of raw materials. The WTO's final ruling in the case was welcomed by the EU's trade chief and business leaders in Europe.

In a statement, China's Ministry of Commerce said it „deeply regrets" the decision but would abide by the ruling, although it considered it had acted legitimately.

The United States, European Union and Mexico had all launched WTO legal cases in 2009, challenging China's right to restrict exports of materials including bauxite, coke, magnesium, manganese and zinc. Many countries also later accused China of choking off global supplies of rare earth metals, causing prices to rocket for crucial ingredients in many high-tech products, but rare earths were not part of Monday's ruling.

China's export restrictions helped to bolster domestic supplies of raw materials, cutting prices for local users. As well as giving an advantage to Chinese industry, it encouraged foreign firms to set up within China to give them a leg-up over competitors who faced higher costs for raw materials.

„Today's report is a tremendous victory for the United States – particularly its manufacturers and workers," US Trade Representative Ron Kirk said in a statement. „The Obama administration will continue to ensure that China and every other country play by the rules so that US workers and companies can compete and succeed on a level playing field."

EU rejoices

EU Trade Commissioner Karel De Gucht said the decision would force China to drop export restrictions for the materials mentioned in the case and for rare earths.

„This final ruling is a great success in our efforts to ensure fair access to the much needed raw materials for EU industry," he said in a statement.

Although China had promised to eliminate export restrictions when it joined the WTO a decade ago, it cited an exemption in WTO rules that allowed it to restrict exports for environmental reasons. But the WTO ruling found that China's terms of accession to the WTO specifically barred it from using the exemption.

The complaints against China were watched by 13 countries, including Brazil, Canada, Norway, Japan and Saudi Arabia, each of which had declared a substantial interest in the outcome to gain observer status in the case.

Euractiv, 31 Jan 2012, https://www.euractiv.com/section/sustainable-dev/news/eu-wins-wto-battle-against-china-over-raw-materials/ (7.7.2017)

Exercises

1. Summarise the most important data points from M 11 – M 13. Who, what, when, and where is the trade dispute about?
2. Prepare a panel discussion in 6 groups to evaluate the trade dispute.
   a. Divide the class into the following six groups: China, the United States, Mexico, the European Union, the WTO panel and a moderation group (that is responsible for procedure and moderation).
   b. Use the information from M 11 - M 17 plus an additional internet research to prepare your case for the panel at the WTO.
   c. Debate the merits of the case independently from the real-life outcome in M 17.
3. Evaluate the importance of the WTO in settling trade disputes based on your experience in class and the information available to you.

4 Final Thoughts on Global Economic Governance

M 1 ● Global Risks and Impact

Top 5 Global Risks in Terms of Likelihood

2013	2014	2015	2016	2017
Severe income disparity	Income disparity	Interstate conflict with regional consequences	Large-scale involuntary migration	Extreme weather events
Chronic fiscal imbalances	Extreme weather events	Extreme weather events	Extreme weather events	Large-scale involuntary migration
Rising greenhouse gas emissions	Unemployment and under-employment	Failure of national governance	Failure of climatechange mitigation and adaption	Major natural disasters
Water supply crises	Climate change	State collapse or crisis	Interstate conflict with regional consequences	Large-scale terrorist attacks
Mismanage-ment of population ageing	Cyber attacks	High structural unemployment or underem-ployment	Major natural catastrophes	Massive incident of data fraud/ theft

Top 5 Global Risks in Terms of Impact

2013	2014	2015	2016	2017
Major systemic financial failure	Fiscal crises	Water crises	Failure of climate-change mitigation and adaptation	Weapons of mass destruction
Water supply crises	Climate change	Rapid and massive spread of infectious diseaseg	Weapons of mass destrucion	Extreme weather events
Chronical fiscal imbalances	Water crises	Weapons of mass destruction	Water crises	Water crises
Diffusion of weapons of mass destruction	Unemployment and under-employment	Interstate conflict with regional consequences	Lange-scale involuntary migration	Major natural disasters
Failure of climate-change mitigation and adaption	Critical information infrastructure breakdown	Failure of climate-change mitigation and adaption	Severe energy price shock	Failure of climate-change mitigation and adaption

■ Economic ■ Environmental ■ Geopolitical ■ Societal ■ Technological

http://reports.weforum.org/global-risks-2017/shareable-infographics/ (23.7.2017)

Jörg Asmussen

discrepancy = gap

pertain = are about the or in regards to

interdependence = when people or countries depend on each other in some or many ways

interconnectedness = when people or countries are connected with each other in some or many ways

unprecedented = never seen or experienced before

tuned = in line with or able to work with

international spillovers = when events in one country or area have an affect on another country or area

M 2 ● The Future of Global Economic Governance

The following speech, "The future of global economic governance" was given by Jörg Asmussen, Member of the Executive Board of the ECB (2012-2013), at Hertie School of Governance, Berlin, 22 February 2013.

It has now become commonplace to say that we live in a "flat world", a world characterised by ever-growing interdependence and interconnectedness. The integration of emerging market economies into the global economy, along with lower transportation costs and technological change has led to unprecedented increases in the circulation of goods, labour, capital and information around the world.

Insofar as the world today has so profoundly changed, it is unsurprising that today's global challenges are also markedly different from those of barely one or two decades ago. The globalisation of production chains is just one example of these profound evolutions. Products are no longer 'made in Germany' or 'made in France'. They are 'made in the world'.

The 2011 natural and nuclear disaster in Japan has shown how much countries are now connected in ways that are far stronger than previously thought. As we have learned, the impairment of a few factories in just one country can have a significant impact on policy choices in other countries, as we see here in Germany, on an entire industry worldwide and, ultimately, on the global economy. [...]

The key question now is whether today's global economic governance is tuned to a world where challenges have become truly global in many aspects, an evolution which the global financial crisis has only accelerated. [...] In my view, despite the important and significant progress already made, global economic governance still falls short of meeting the scale of today's challenges.

First and foremost this is because it is still largely driven by national considerations, but also because the evolutions that have occurred since the crisis still leave some key issues unresolved. These pertain to the leadership, coherence, efficiency and legitimacy of global economic governance. The discrepancy between the reality of today's interdependences, the challenges they create, and the capacity of sovereign governments to agree on how to deal with them remains significant. [...]

Any meaningful collective decision that helps address pressing global policy issues requires a consensus between sovereign nations, which still results from – often difficult – compromises. Global economic relations hence remain mostly inter-national rather than transnational or supranational. [...] It crucially depends on the ability of sovereign nations to find consensual solutions to the common challenges they face and on their willingness to stick to their agreements.

Within the G20, for instance, advanced economies cannot be forced to implement the commitments they made at the Toronto Summit of 2010 [...] if they are reluctant to do so. Nor can emerging market economies be forced to move more rapidly towards market-based exchange rates.

Even in global trade relations, which are policed by WTO rules, the preferred solution in case of disputes is not to resort to the WTO's system of dispute settlement, but for the countries concerned to discuss their problems and settle disputes by themselves. [...] The 2008 global financial and economic crisis has made more visible the gap between power and politics created by globalisation. As interdependences and international spillovers have steadily grown, power, i.e. the ability to address today's most pressing policy challenges, such as international macroeconomic cooperation, global imbalances, financial regulatory reform or protectionism has partly evaporated from the Nation-State to the global level. But politics [...] remains largely local and national, as it was before. [...]

Global economic governance [...] has become more inclusive, notably through the ascent of the G20. It has been reformed to account for the growing importance of emerging market economies in the global economy. [...]
Hence global economic governance as we know it today seems to be well equipped to manage a global crisis. But it is less effective during normal times, which also lessens its ability to prevent future crises. [...]
Moreover, there is no shortage of global challenges in need of a global response, just think of trade and protectionism, the still not completed financial reform agenda or climate change. [...]
To conclude, the 2008 global and financial crisis has shown the need for more global solutions. Global leaders have shown their ability to respond to this need. Looking ahead, the work is not completed. It is now entirely up to all of us to keep the momentum going [...].

Jörg Asmussen, https://www.ecb.europa.eu/press/key/date/2013/html/sp130222_1.en.html (12.7.2017)

ascent = start of and rising importance of

Exercises

1. Describe how the global risks and their impacts have changed in the past 5 years. What similarities and differences are there (M 1)?
2. Comment on which risks and impacts you think are most relevant for the future. Are there risks and impacts missing (M 1)?
3. Outline the future global economic governance challenges that Jörg Assmussen talks about in his speech (M 2).
4. Assess the challenges made by Jörg Assmussen. Do you agree or disagree with his outlook on the future of global economic governance?

1. Agreeing
I agree with ...
I couldn't agree more ...
You're absolutely right there ...
I can see your point ...
You're right up to a point ...
Exactly ...
I can understand ...

2. Disagreeing
You're missing the point ...
I totally disagree with ...
That's all very well, but ...
You may not believe it, but
I can't accept ...
Wouldn't it be better to ...
I see what you mean, but
I see your point, but I think ...
Yes, but on the other hand ...
I'm not with you there ...
What I object to is ...
I (very much) doubt whether ...
That can't be right!
Never!

3. Clarifying
Absolutely right, but ...
Let us focus on this issue here ...
What has that got to do with ...
Have you thought of ...
Let me give you another example ...
I don't see what you mean ...
You must admit that ...
Do you realize ...
What do you mean by ...
So you are saying that ...
The main priority is ...
Why do you say that ...
Well, it depends on ...
Is there any reason why ...
Do you really mean to say that ...
Let me put this clear ...
It may sound strange but ...

4. Giving an opinion
My feeling is ...
What I'm concerned with is ...
I hold the view that ...
If you ask me ...
An additional argument I would like to present is that ...
I'm pretty sure that ...
My personal view is that ...
In my experience ...
Personally, I think/believe/suppose ...
The surprising thing is that ...
I'm fairly certain that ...
I'm convinced that ...
To my mind ...
In my opinion/ I'm of the opinion ...
The fact of the matter is ...
It is my firm believe that ...
The way I see it ...

5. Giving in
What I like about this argument/thought is ...
I take that back ...
There is some common ground between us here ...
I think we can draw the following conclusion ...
I have never thought of/about that before ...
I see things in a different light now ...
I can see your point ...
I must admit that ...

6. Interrupting
I'm sorry, but ...
Excuse me, can/may I add something?
Sorry to interrupt, but ...
Just listen for a moment ...
I am trying to answer your question ...
As I have said it before ...
Do you mind if I jump in here?
Pardon me ...
I don't mean to intrude ...

- © 2015 / IW Medien / iwd 39, Köln – S. 22
- © 2015 / IW Medien / IW-Pressemitteilung englisch 30.03.2015, Köln – S. 28
- Amorim / Cartoonmovement, Haarlem – S. 30
- © Automotive News Europe 2017, München – S. 23
- Khalil Bendib / www.bendib.com / All rights reserved, Berkeley – S. 11
- © Chappatte in The International Herald Tribune / www.chappatte.com – S. 34
- dpa-infografik / Globus-Grafik, Frankfurt – S. 9
- dpa Picture-Alliance / AP Photo / Elias Meseret, Frankfurt – S. 18; - / Arved Gintenreiter – S. 7; - / Marthe van der Wolf – S. 25
- Getty Images / AFP / Patrik Stollarz / Staff – S. 7; - / Bloomberg / Kevin Lee – Cover, S. 7
- The Global Competitiveness Report / World Economic Forum, Switzerland 2016-2017 – S. 21
- thinkstock / Hemera – Cover; - / iStock / zanskar – Cover
- Matt Wuerker, Washington D. C. – S. 5
- www.wikimedia.org – S. 26
- www.wikimedia.org / Martin Jost / CC BY-SA 3.0 – S. 44
- www.wikimedia.org / Ricardo Stuckert / ABr / CC BY-SA 3.0 BR – S. 6
- www.wikimedia.org / Robert D. Ward – S. 6
- www.wikimedia.org / Elke Wetzig (Elya) / CC BY-SA 3.0 – S. 6
- www.wikipedia.de / Jonathan McItosh – S. 7